Dancing in the Family

Dancing in the Family

An Unconventional Memoir of Three Women

Sukanya Rahman

For Mancy + Leonard
Super dance enthusiast!
With much love
Sukanya
2002

HarperCollins *Publishers* India

HarperCollins *Publishers* India Pvt. Ltd
7/16 Ansari Road, Daryaganj, New Delhi 110 002

First published in 2001 by
HarperCollins *Publishers* India

ISBN 81-7223-438-4

Typeset by
Nikita Overseas Pvt. Ltd
19A Ansari Road, Daryaganj
New Delhi 110 002

Printed in India by
Rekha Printers Pvt. Ltd
A-102/1 Okhla Industrial Area,
New Delhi 110 020

For
Habib and Wardreath

How does it all begin? I suppose it never begins, it just continues—Life—generations dancing.

Martha Graham

Contents

Acknowledgements

My deep gratitude to all who helped make this dream a reality: to Peggy Cowles for her generous support and for her faith in me; The National Endowment for the Arts, and the John Anson Kittredge Educational Trust for their generous financial support; members of the Brunswick River Road Writer's Group for giving me the courage to persevere; Pam Mensch, Camilla Wood, Bonnie Brooks, Aditya Behl, Sanjiv Saith, and Lochi and Nat Glazer for their insightful comments at the various stages of my project; Martin McDonough of the Mt. Ararat High School computer centre for his patience and technical expertise; Jack Hawley, Amitav Ghosh, Debbie Baker, Marina Budhos and Walter Harper for their generous efforts in helping me find a home for this book; Sunil Kothari, Lalit Mansingh, Ashish Khokar, Gina Blau, Maria Moya, Litia Namoura, Doris Norden Chattopadhyaya, Leonard Gordon, Tapan Mukherjee, Mariam Ghosh Sherar, Zarina Rahman, Altaf Rahman and Rang Vittal for their invaluable assistance, large and small, in editiorial guidance; Renuka Chatterjee, my editor at HarperCollins, for giving this book a home; my brother, Ram, for helping with the photographs and for keeping me striving; my friend and fiercest critic, Laura, for graciously prodding and piloting me and for talking me out of chucking my manuscript into a bonfire; and finally, to my husband and equally fierce critic, Frank, for his support, endurance and eternal optimism.

Preface

$\mathcal{I}$n 1982, some months after the death of my grandmother, Ragini Devi, my mother handed over to me for safekeeping her mother's most precious possessions. Stuffed into several large shopping bags, bearing the names of an assortment of New York City stores, were bulky photo albums, Bible records of the Parker/Abbott families dating back to 1660, Ragini's certificate of marriage to my grandfather, a collection of expired passports, old affidavits, documents, and a few personal letters. Sifting through the contents, many years later, one of the letters, addressed to a "Mrs. Bradley," grabbed my attention. Written from Bangalore on 19 February 1931, the three-page letter described in detail my grandmother's journey to India, a broken love affair, and the birth of my mother, Indrani.

Much of the information in the letter I was already familiar with. Over the years, my mother, who was a marvellous storyteller, had entertained family and friends with outrageous anecdotes of growing up with her strong, independent, unconventional mother who had dragged her across the world, and raised her to become a dance superstar. It was in reading the Bradley letter that I was struck for the first time by the sheer bravura of a woman who had broken down all barriers in pursuit of a dream.

By the time I came to know my grandmother she was quite matronly, retired from the stage, and struggling to complete her second book on Indian dance. The great-grandmother my two sons remember was a stooped-over old lady who lived in a nursing home in New Jersey, but was still savvy enough to send them masks at Halloween depicting the rock group Kiss and other current pop icons. I wanted to bring back to life for my children this other Ragini—the beautiful, indomitable young dancer who had poured her heart out to Mrs. Bradley.

To sort out fact from fiction, and out of sheer curiosity, I had tried probing my grandmother with questions in her lifetime. But she was always cagey. It was virtually impossible to penetrate the persona she had created.

To piece her life together I began by re-reading her first book, *Nritanjali,* in which I uncovered valuable insights into Ragini's intellectual persona. From the introduction and conclusion of her second book, *Dance Dialects of India,* I learned more about her early passion for dance, for India, and her professional touring days. But even there my mother had to help me ferret out the facts. I pored over microfilms of Ragini's reviews, articles and programmes that my mother had donated to the Library for the Performing Arts at Lincoln Center. I came across articles at the New York Public Library. I crawled under the bed in our Delhi flat and extracted, from an ancient dust-covered suitcase, crumbling, yellowed newspaper clippings dating back to 1926. I tracked down Ragini's friends and colleagues. In Delhi, I tried to get Kamaladevi Chattopadhyaya to talk about the woman who had run off with her husband, but she was just as cagey as my grandmother and would keep changing the subject. She would only say that she had great respect for Ragini as an artist, and remembered her as a beautiful dancer with especially expressive abhinaya.

Ragini's story is also the story of three generations of women that continues down through my mother and myself. Happily, unravelling my mother's early life was much easier since she was a lively, nonstop talker. She recalled stories and anecdotes when we chatted over the phone. Strolling with her, along some street in New York's Greenwich Village would trigger dormant memories. One evening, when I was visiting my mother in her East Village apartment in New York, we were polishing off a bottle of Bordeaux and eating Chinese takeout while watching TV. Jessye Norman, the incomparable diva, was singing the *Liebestod* aria from the opera, *Tristan and Isolde*. It set off a flood of nostalgia, and my mother began to reminisce about her early romance with my father when she was barely fourteen.

I had a vast collection of interviews my mother had given over the course of her career, both on tape and in print. While I drew from these, they seemed to me somewhat self-conscious and guarded. It was the little unsolicited nugget she would throw out at unexpected moments that brought her story to life for me. I recorded these by scribbling on backs of envelopes and scraps of paper. Of course each time she repeated a story it was a little different, so whenever possible I tried to view each incident from other angles. When I visited my father in Delhi, we would talk late into the night, with American soap operas flickering on the TV.

There were stories, especially about the beauty contest, my mother didn't want me to tell. Then one day, in the mail, I received from her pictures of herself parading in a bathing suit with other international beauties!

Those voices, those images, and the shopping bags bulging with my grandmother's precious possessions, are my legacies to my sons.

Sukanya Rahman
Orr's Island, Maine

1

Rehearsal

ance was a family obsession. There was no escaping it. It was
our religion. Dance came first.

When my grandmother did something grandmotherly, like
take me to the circus, she would embarrass me horribly by
demonstrating dance steps along the sidewalk. My father, a
distinguished architect by profession, would cap off each dinner
party at our Calcutta flat with an imitation of the American modern
dancer, Martha Graham. My mother, when she wasn't travelling all
over the country studying or performing, would convert our drawing
room into a rehearsal studio. And my grandfather, whom I had not
yet met, would write to me often from New York, urging me not to
become a dancer.

While I secretly prayed my family would become normal, I did
love the daily spectacle of our domestic life. Instead of joining the
neighbourhood children for games of hide 'n seek or hopscotch, I

preferred to amuse myself on the veranda, where I'd idle away many happy hours, on the lookout for the odd assortment of characters who wandered in and out of our flat with regularity.

I remember one stiflingly warm afternoon when Guru Sukhdev Maharaj made his appearance on Lower Circular Road; a vision in orange, growing larger and larger as he marched along under his sturdy black umbrella. He staggered up the three flights of stairs leading into our flat and declared to no one in particular, "Arre baap re baap! So very, very hot today!"

Still huffing and puffing, he propped his umbrella against the wall, removed his orange tennis shoes by the door and then, with the sleeve of his flowing saffron robe, wiped the beads of perspiration off his glistening bald head, and patted the stray strands of his scraggly white beard into place.

My mother rushed up to greet her dance teacher. She touched his feet, led him into the drawing room, switched on the ceiling fan, pushed the few pieces of furniture against the walls and dispatched me to the kitchen to fetch a cold lemon squash. Guruji settled down on a mat at one end of the room and after a few gulps of lemon squash and a good burp, punctuated by a satisfied "Om," regained his composure.

The old dance master then rolled up his sleeves, took a small metal hammer out of his shoulder bag and tuned the pair of tablas set before him. He sprinkled some Johnson's Baby Powder on his hands, and finally with a nod of his head indicated he was ready. My mother tucked the palloo of her magenta cotton sari into her waist and twisted her hair into a knot; she touched the floor and bowed to her teacher with palms joined in a namaskar. Then with one arm folded over the other, she slowly stamped out the basic rhythms he played on the drums.

Her gliding neck movements, fluttering eyebrows, rapid spins and intricate footwork brought to life the quickening rhythms of the drums. I sat on the mat beside this flaming orange Santa Claus, mesmerised at how far his spit could fly as he recited the dance bols:

"Ta tai tai tat—ta tai tai tat—tat tat thun thun—
Ti ta thigi thigi tai . . ."

I was soon distracted by the sound of people fighting on the street below; traces of a foreign accent singled out one of the louder voices. I ran to the veranda and spotted my grandmother arguing with a rickshaw-wallah. Nani was resplendent in a green silk sari bordered with gold brocade; heavy golden jhumkas pulled her ear lobes down; an embroidered, mirrored purse dangled from her wrist. She stood on the pavement with both hands planted defiantly on her hips, and her glass bangles jingled as she raised an arm and gesticulated to me, "Ayah ko bulau, Ayah ko bulau!"

Our ayah came running through the drawing room out to the veranda and started screaming at the rickshaw-wallah. There seemed to be a dispute over the fare. Ayah motioned my grandmother to come up. She wrapped two four-anna coins in a piece of paper and threw it to the rickshaw-wallah. He picked up the money, pulled his rickshaw, and went off grumbling. The small crowd that had collected, hoping to participate in a good fight, dispersed in disappointment.

Before my mother could get back to her lesson the front door flew open, and Nani—triumphant over her battle with the rickshaw-wallah—swept into the room. I chewed my nails down to the skin, convinced Mummy would explode at all these interruptions. But Guru Sukhdev Maharaj, eager to show his pupil off, rushed up to greet my grandmother, and invited her to sit on the mat beside us.

The tuberoses tucked into the bun at the nape of her neck were wilting as was her legendary beauty. She took a lipstick out of her purse, puckered her lips and painted them a bright red; a faint scent of Max Factor make-up, that was beginning to cake around her mouth, lingered over her. She squinted her kohl-darkened eyes and followed my mother's every move.

Her plan was to have my mother study Bharata Natyam, the elegant feminine style of dance that had evolved in the temples of South India centuries earlier. But in the late 1940s, the few teachers of Bharata Natyam living in Calcutta were scared away by the riots that had erupted in the wake of Partition and India's independence from Britain, and had fled back to South India.

In the meantime, rather than not dance at all, my mother chose to study Kathak, the courtly dance form of North India, with Sukhdev Maharaj, a renowned guru who was residing in Calcutta at the time.

"Ti ta kata gadhi ghana ta—ti ta kata gadhi ghana ta—
Ti ta kata gadhi ghana ta . . ."

The more enthusiastic the guru became, the further his spit flew—his umbrella, I imagined, could be put to better use now . . . Daddy returned from the office and quietly slipped into the drawing room to catch the last few moments of Mummy's class. She ended it with a brilliant display of paltas, spiral turns and a final stamp of the right foot.

My father helped push the furniture back where it belonged, and after settling into a low wooden chowki, he inserted two fingers in his mouth and produced a shrill whistle.

"Ji huzoor!" came the immediate answer from the kitchen. Moments later, her sari now demurely over her head, Ayah returned carrying the tea tray. Added to the usual assortment of Britannia biscuits were spongy white rasagullas, sizzling vegetable pakoras and fresh mint chutney. Ayah slammed the tray down on the table, and on her way out of the room complained to the world at large in her screechy blend of Bengali and Urdu:

"Do we run a hotel here or what? How am I supposed to stretch the bazaar money if I have to feed every pest who comes off the street?"

I popped several sweet juicy rasagullas into my mouth. Mummy poured the tea while my grandmother chatted, in a hodgepodge of Hindi and English, with Sukhdev Maharaj and caught up with the world of Kathak dance. His prize pupils, his daughter Sitara Devi and nephew Gopi Krishna, both flamboyant performers and popular exponents of the art, were busy touring and performing. Nani probed further. Was it true he was living in Calcutta's red-light district? Yes, yes, that was correct. Until recently, he had been attached to the palace in Nepal, teaching dance and music. He returned to Calcutta with a group of baijis from the royal court. Teaching the dancing girls sacred Hindu dances, he was certain, would elevate their respectability and social status.

Nani passed around some freshly fried onion pakoras, but deliberately ignored my father. When their eyes accidentally met she quickly rearranged the expression on her face into one of self-pity and hurt pride. Truce had not yet been declared between them. A few nights earlier, as a joke, my father had replaced a bottle of gin with an identical bottle filled with water, knowing, once he and my mother went out for the evening, his mother-in-law would head straight for it.

Nani was literally camping with us. She slept in the drawing room on a folding cot, and each morning the aroma of her coffee, mingled with the penetrating odour of the bidis she enjoyed smoking, permeated through the flat. Her costume trunk, with "R.D. New York City" stamped on top, was stored in the hallway—still waiting to be opened.

2

Esther Luella

y grandmother, as I knew her, was the creation of Esther Luella Sherman who was born by some mistake of nature into an American family in Petoskey, Michigan, on 18 August 1893. That was the date recorded in the family Bible. According to her own records, the date fluctuated anywhere between 1896 and 1905. As she grew older, she became more creative with the dates and would knock twenty or twenty-five years off her age without any qualms, then wait for reactions of belief or disbelief.

She also generally avoided divulging her American roots or the fact that she had grown up in Minneapolis. Her parents, Ida and Alex Sherman, had moved and settled in that city while she and her younger brother, Otto DeWitt, were still children. They were raised in an unimposing, white clapboard house on a quiet tree-lined street by the shores of Lake Harriet. An average, conventional and close-knit family, they traced their heritage to the founding fathers of America.

Esther's mother, Ida Bell Parker, was descended from the families of James Abbott, of Somersetshire, England, who came and settled near Hempstead, Long Island about 1690, and Joshua Parker, born in Delaware County, New York, in 1773. James Abbott's grandson, Reverend Benjamin Abbott was a celebrated Methodist preacher on Long Island and in New Jersey; while another James Abbott, of Huntington, New York, gained notoriety by refusing to sign the Association Test of 1775, boycotting British goods and services. The Parker branch of the family settled at Parker's Corners in 1835, and according to family tradition the Liberty Bell was rung on the Parker's farm in Parkersburg, Virginia. Ida Bell Parker's uncles, Burdick Abbott and Hiram Chase, distinguished themselves fighting in the Civil War.

Esther's father, Alexander Otto Sherman, was a second-generation American born of German parents in Newstead, near Hanover, Ontario. A tall man of aristocratic demeanour, he was a cutter and designer of gentlemen's clothes and tailored some of the finest suits worn by the men of Minneapolis. He was in business for himself for many years until he retired. Retirement, he found, was unsuited to his temperament and he went back into business at age seventy, and with his son, DeWitt, operated the Sherman and Son Tailor Shop in downtown Minneapolis where he continued till the age of ninety-two, when he finally sold his business.

DeWitt, an automotive engineer by profession, was incapacitated by poison gas during World War I and received a medal for bravery at the battle of Verdun in 1918. Although he later married, he lived a semi-retired life and never left his parents' home. Both avid fishermen, Alex Sherman and DeWitt spent all their spare time fishing the lakes of Minnesota; it was a hobby and sport they never tired of. Alex Sherman enjoyed people and entertaining as well. An excellent "500" card player, he played cards till the last years of his life.

Ida Parker was primarily a homemaker, yet she was artistic with her hands, and both she and her husband were also amateur musicians who enjoyed giving impromptu recitals, performing the music of Bach, Brahms and Beethoven on the piano and violin for friends and family in the parlour of their home.

Their music inspired Esther to dance. As a child of eight she would slip out of the house after dark when she heard music and dance barefoot on the lawn, dressed in old Halloween costumes and fancy dresses pulled from trunks stored in the attic. Her dancing was free and untutored; when there was no music she would hum any tune that came to mind and dance. She was about twelve when a cousin, who belonged to a boys' amateur theatre group, was given the part of a dancing girl in a play. He enrolled in a dance school to prepare for the role and came back and taught Esther what he had learned. Impressed by her abilities, he brought the dance teacher to the house to give her formal lessons. She went on to continue her training in ballet with Ivan Tarasoff, a ballet master from Russia; she studied voice and musical theory; and after completing high school, enrolled in art classes at the Walker Art Center.

She led a lively social life centred around costume parties, picnics, sailing, swimming, even hydroplane rides. In the summer of 1912, she won first prize at the Lake Harriet Canoe Carnival riding a canoe her mother had decorated with crepe paper flowers to resemble a Dutch windmill. She enjoyed enormous popularity among her friends who thought she resembled the film star, Gloria Swanson.

While in her teens, she teamed up with a local Russian dancer and devised a programme of international dances. Before long she and her partner were performing their Russian folk dances, Cossack dances, a "Mazurka Militaire," and dainty Skirt dances in small cabarets and theatres in and around Minneapolis. Calling herself "Rita Cassilas" she spiced up the repertoire with her own solo numbers, costumed at times as a lissome Greek nymph, a sultry Egyptian, and as "Todi Ragini."

These performances generally kept her out late and had her mother sick with worry. The family had little exposure to anything foreign and found it hard to comprehend their daughter's increasingly eccentric fascination for the exotic. One cold blustery night the Russian delivered her back home later than usual. As punishment, Alex Sherman refused to let his daughter into the house and left her shivering on the sidewalk. Respectable young women, in his opinion, did not stay out all night with strange men, especially foreign men who danced. In desperation, the Russian ran down the road and reported the situation to a policeman patrolling the area. The officer calmed him down and assured him there wouldn't be any need for the young lady to spend the night at the police station or in a hotel. The policeman accompanied the young man back to the house, pounded on the front door and, shouting roughly, ordered the father to take his daughter in. Neighbours switched on their lights. Dogs started to bark. It was the greatest excitement the normally staid neighbourhood had ever experienced.

Shortly after this incident Esther—now considered the black sheep of the family—attached herself to the small community of young expatriates from India at the University of Minnesota at Saint Paul, soaking up everything they knew of their literature, music and dance. She began to listen to gramophone records of Indian classical music, she sought out books on Indian art and sculpture from libraries and began to study the forms. She spent her days closeted at the university library, devouring books on India. She came across two ancient Sanskrit texts, the *Natya Shastra* and the *Abhinaya Darpana*, containing chapters that provided detailed descriptions of hand gestures, intricate footwork, facial expressions and sentiments of classical Indian dance. One of her teachers, a Sanskrit scholar, translated these for her into English. She studied these texts, absorbed the music, analysed the sculpture and paintings, and drawing on these resources, began to create her own "Indian" dance movements.

At the university, she met Ramlal Balaram Bajpai, a chemistry student from India. Like many Indians at the university, Bajpai, a Hindu Brahmin, was a political refugee, wanted by the ruling British in India for sedition. As a student activist, back in his hometown in Nagpur, he had been fighting to overthrow the British. Late one night, he and a group of his fellow revolutionaries defiled a larger-than-life bronze statue of Queen Victoria by urinating on it. They pulled the statue down, dragged it some distance, disfigured it with tar, and then dumped it into a lotus pond in the middle of the city. A traitor within the group provided the names of each student to the British authorities, and a warrant for the arrest of all those involved was immediately issued. The penalty for this act of "treason" was death by hanging. That same night, Bajpai went underground. The next day, without

saying goodbye to his mother, whom he never saw again, he was
smuggled out of the city with help from the Hindu Mahasabha party,
with which he was affiliated, and eventually shipped off via Calcutta
to Japan. In Japan a well-established group, actively working for
India's Independence Movement, prepared false documents for him.
They had ties with the University of Minnesota and the encouragement
of progressive Minnesotans like Hubert Humphrey. Ramlal Bajpai
was one of the earliest Indian patriots to come to America to seek
political and financial support and sympathy for India's struggle
for freedom.

Shortly after he graduated from the university, Esther followed
him to New York City where they continued their friendship; and
after a brief courtship and against her parents' wishes, or consent,
she accepted Bajpai's proposal of marriage and married him on 21
May 1921 in a quiet, civil ceremony in Wilmington, Delaware.

Her passion for dance did not fade away with matrimony as
Bajpai, who had little interest in the arts, had hoped. Her husband
was her passport to the Indian community in New York. Through
his social and political milieu, she was brought into close association
with Indian artists and Indian musicians living in New York or passing
through the city.

Orientalism was all the rage in the early twenties. Socialites in
Boston and New York dabbled in Eastern mysticism and philosophy.
Prima ballerina Anna Pavlova, after her tour to India, was inspired
to create ballets with Indian themes; Nijinsky manifested himself as
the Blue God; and Ruth St. Denis captivated audiences with exotic
and decorative ballets that exuded an Indian aura.

Encouraged by this vogue, Esther launched into organising her
solo performances. She rehearsed her dances, hired a professional
studio to shoot publicity pictures, and became her own impresario.
At the time there was little knowledge in America about authentic
classical Indian dance. Her mission was to change that. She believed
dance and music, one of the finest phases of Hindu life, must not
be allowed to remain unknown to the world. "The world should
know of it, and the great masters should ponder over the possibility
of its revival and renovation for the whole world . . . Some people

who love Hindu music and dancing must give their lives to it. I love India and I am trying to find the beauty of my life through Hindu music and dancing to which I have consecrated my life."

She came to understand that Indian dance was an act of worship and not for entertainment. To reveal the spiritual beauty of the art, she believed, one had to be Indian. She set out to transform herself entirely, and in a sense became the music that drew her to India: the ragas and the raginis. She began to call herself Sri Ragini, then Ragini Devi. Since her marriage, she had taken to wearing saris. She wore her dark brown hair parted in the middle, marked her forehead with a spot of vermilion, and darkened her skin with "Indian mud."

Her transformation was total. In an interview that was published in *The American Weekly* in 1926, she told a reporter that she was a girl of Kashmir, a high-caste Brahmin, who had spent much of her childhood in the secret sanctuaries of India and Tibet, studying the invisible dances and inaudible music of Tibet—dancing that cannot be seen by the untrained eye and music that cannot be heard by the untrained ear.

The invisible dance, she said, was based on velocity: lamas of Tibet leap and gyrate so fast that the eye can't follow them. Dancers move their hands and feet forty times a second—a speed which the ordinary human eye is unable to register. Untrained eyes get a blurred impression, the effect of floating. Inaudible music is based on velocity of pitch. Sounds that others hear as a mere whisper, a Tibetan lama hears plainly; his ear is accustomed to the silence of an altitude of 15,000 feet. Ordinary humans lack the sixth sense.

"It's not surprising when you think it over," she said. "Play Beethoven's Fifth Symphony to your dog, and he hears nothing but a jumble of sound. He doesn't react. His ear isn't educated to that sort of sound."

When she first arrived in America, Ragini Devi said to the reporter, she was amazed to discover that singers and dancers performed their art for a fee. "In Tibet and in most parts of the Orient generally," she explained, "all public performances are free of charge and take place mostly in temples or courtyards of private houses. Singers and dancers are treated as favoured guests and heaped with gifts. Once my presents at a concert in Mongolia consisted of six camels and fifteen sheep which I had to take with me for fear of giving offence to my host."

Any doubt on the veracity of these claims vanished from the reporter's mind after he attended her performance of invisible dances. "In order to convince the sceptical audience that her account of the invisible dance was not exaggerated," he wrote in *The American Weekly*, "Ragini Devi performs a fantastically beautiful number she calls 'Dance of Krishna.' She does this dance in a manner which proves the truth of her contention that the dance is invisible. Onlookers who witnessed the dance were unable to count the rhythmic movements of her hands and feet, and got only an impression of Ragini Devi floating about the room."

3

Ragini Devi

The Bajpai apartment at 209 Sullivan Place in Brooklyn became a gathering place for Indian émigrés, and their nationalist and political activities—a hotbed for the Independence Movement. Ragini was, by now, resigned to her husband sharing his roof and his purse with indigent political refugees from India. He was working full time for his political mentor, Lala Lajpat Rai—the nationalist leader and champion of India Home Rule. As a councillor of the India Home Rule League, Bajpai had been thrust into the centre of nationalist activities. From the time it was founded in New York in 1915 by Lala Lajpat Rai, the Home Rule League had attracted the attention of British intelligence agents operating in America. Its office at 1400 Broadway was constantly under surveillance. Radical nationalists, in an ultimate act of opposition to Britain, had sided with Germany during World War I. Several Indians, and American sympathisers of Indians, like Dr. Taraknath Das, Sailendra Ghosh and Agnes Smedly, suspected of being a part of a "German-Hindu conspiracy" and a "Hindu-Bolshevik clique," were picked up and deported or imprisoned at the jail known as Tombs in downtown Manhattan.

Young India, a monthly journal brought out by the more moderate Home Rule League, was now being used successfully to lobby Congressional support for India's cause in Washington. Quarrels, which frequently arose between more militant factions of Indian groups and institutions, were usually arbitrated by Bajpai, who had a reputation for being a brilliant, fair and kind mediator.

Ragini, married to Bajpai now for almost ten years, had established herself as a respected authority on Indian dance and music. In 1928 she wrote *Nritanjali*, the first book on Indian dance to be published in English. Based on her studies of *The Mirror of Gesture* by Ananda Coomaraswamy, some translations from the *Natya Shastra,* and her own dances, this small book simply and eloquently sought to unravel the spiritual complexities and intricacies of the classical Indian dance vocabulary for the uninitiated. Critical acclaim of the book had made a name for her both in America and in India.

"Sadly enough, to us the phrase 'Oriental dancing' has pretty generally brought up little else than the picture of the '*danse du ventre*' which was for many years the particularly spicy feature of every carnival or fair from Maine to California," wrote John Martin, dance critic of *The New York Times*. ". . . it is, therefore, a happy circumstance that there should be a few devotees like Ragini who are able not only to perform the classic dances but also to write about them in such a form that we of the West may acquire some appreciation of them before they disappear from the earth."

And *The Dancing Times*, London, wrote: "It is difficult to study dancing of all arts, from a book: yet expert guidance, accurate description, and careful explanations . . . are offered in this valuable volume by Sri Ragini. It carries its own commendation upon every page being the work of an artist for artists."

Ragini was now sought after among both wide and select circles of the public for her lively, illuminating programmes of Indian dance and music. Audiences responded enthusiastically to her interpretations of ancient and modern dances of India's gods and goddesses. With structured rhythmic development, graceful hand gestures and facial expressions, she communicated to audiences the charm and vivacity of the divine flute player, Krishna, and his beloved, Radha.

She toured the country with two colourfully costumed North Indian musicians who accompanied her dances. In 1928 she booked this "Trio Ragini" into the Booth Theatre on Broadway for a series of performances which sold out. *The New York Times* described the performance as "an exotic evening of East Indian music at the Booth Theatre last night, marked by half lights of subtle atmospheric suggestion and by highlights of appealing lyric beauty. The songs and dances of Ragini won her audience with simple truth of graceful interpretation rare to be seen in the theatre. Several of Ragini's numbers had to be repeated, beautiful plastic poses accompanied by sinuous serpentine movements of the arms and hands."

Her husband, meanwhile, had given up a lucrative job with a pharmaceutical company in order to devote his time to Lala Lajpat Rai and the freedom movement, often travelling across the country to raise funds for the cause. For Ragini, this led to a variety of experiences since she was constantly devising ways to augment her income. She appeared in Carnegie Hall in a prologue to *The Light of Asia*, Himanshu Roy and Devika Rani's film based on Edwin Arnold's poem on the life of Buddha. The film received a lukewarm reception, but Ragini's brief song and devotional dance, invoking Shiva, created a stir. "Sri Ragini is a native of India," wrote one American critic. "She is as naturally imbued with the traditions of her country as any other artist who ever entered this country . . . Ragini Devi has a truly beautiful voice, a mysterious manner of intoning her songs, and with a sensuous style of dance to add to the atmosphere."

Ragini sang as a soloist with Leopold Stokowski's Philadelphia Orchestra. She was named head of the Music and Dance chair at the Nicholas Roerich Museum on Riverside Drive. She shared a double bill with the popular American entertainer/cowboy Will Rogers, and appeared in small parts in silent movies filmed in Astoria, Queens, and across the river in Fort Lee, New Jersey.

A lecture on Indian art by Dr. James Cousins, an Irish poet and theosophist who had made his home in South India, further ignited

Ragini's interest in Indian dance. Included in the slides illustrating his talk were pictures of a rare form of Indian dance drama, Kathakali, which he lamented was languishing in the villages of Kerala on the southwest coast of India. Ostracised by the ruling British, these sacred temple dance traditions were now threatened with extinction.

Ragini had a long discussion with Dr. Cousins about Kathakali, and learned also about the plight of the Devadasis who were banned from dancing in the temples because of social prejudice. She talked with him about her desire to go to South India to study classical dance and learn the authentic ancient forms from the great masters while they were still living. Dr. Cousins assured her it would be possible, and encouraged her in her plans to give dance performances in India to finance her stay. But Ramlal Bajpai had misgivings: besides being financially unrealistic, it would be impractical since he could not accompany Ragini to his homeland—he was still wanted by the British for treason.

While Bajpai tried to show Ragini support in her art by helping her sell tickets to her performances to his friends and colleagues, he was, at the same time, embarrassed to see his wife display herself before the public. Dancing and singing for an audience of intimate friends in the privacy of their home, he thought, was one thing, but dancing for complete strangers was quite another.

He made the greatest mistake of his life when he invited a fellow nationalist from India to stay at the Brooklyn apartment. Harindranath Chattopadhyaya was a handsome and youthful Indian Marxist, poet, musician, dramatist and cultural representative of the political movement in India, crusading to revive traditional Indian theatre. His political connections were hefty: his older sister Sarojini Naidu was a nationalist leader and assistant of Mahatma Gandhi. His brother Virendra, now living in Berlin, was a leading Indian revolutionist allied with the Germans during World War I. Chattopadhyaya's wife, Kamala Devi, was also a leading nationalist, ardent feminist, and early champion of India's cottage industries.

From the moment Ragini and Harin set eyes on each other sparks began to fly. He recited his latest poems to her, he sang songs he had composed, and he urged her to dance for him. His mischievous dark eyes burned right through her. He would take her away to India, he whispered behind Bajpai's back. Ragini was swept off her feet. She couldn't think straight. Were Harin's promises sincere, or were they dalliances of a slightly drunken admirer?

Harin had grand plans for Ragini. He offered to organise dance tours for her across the country to finance her studies with the great gurus. He immediately shot off letters and began to contact impresarios in India. He even talked of establishing a dance centre in Hyderabad, where his sister had a home.

In April 1930, more than two hundred members and guests of the India Society of America gathered at a glittering dinner at the Town Hall Club in Harin's honour. Dinner was followed by the presentation of a $1,000 purse dedicated to support Harin's work in India. In accepting the gift, Harin said he hoped that his New Theatre Movement would form a strong link between India and the United States. He attributed the decline of art in India to "disturbed political and economic conditions as well as to an education from the West wholly unsuited to that country."

While Bajpai was away on one of his frequent trips to California's San Joaquin Valley, seeking contributions for the freedom movement from the large and generous population of Sikh immigrants who had settled there, Ragini and Harin quietly sold all the furniture in the Brooklyn apartment and moved out. Some weeks later, on a fine day in May, they boarded a ship headed for Cherbourg, France. Amid all the chaos Ragini had left the trunk containing all her stage costumes and most of her clothing in the Brooklyn apartment. Harin was supposed to have collected the trunk. Instead, he left it in charge of friends who promised to send it on to them. By the time Bajpai returned and discovered what had taken place it was too late. He did, however, trace the friends who had the trunk and took possession of it.

Despite this setback, and the misfortune of losing a hundred dollars, Ragini and Harin celebrated their "elopement" with a blissful honeymoon in Paris. They dined in sidewalk cafés, strolled down the grand boulevards hand in hand, visited the gardens and palaces of Versailles and Fontainebleau.

Harin then sailed ahead to Colombo in Ceylon to make necessary arrangements. Some ten days later Ragini boarded a French ship from Marseilles for the voyage to Colombo. When her ship anchored in Colombo, Ragini was in for a rude shock. British officers came on board looking for her and confiscated her passport.

In his anguish over his wife's desertion, Ramlal Bajpai had apparently alerted the immigration authorities to her dubious political connections, and to some discrepancies in her passport. At that time Americans who married Asians automatically lost their US citizenship. They later returned her passport to her, but would not permit her to leave the ship and go ashore.

Harin had promised to meet Ragini in Colombo and entertain her for the day before she continued on to Madras, where he would eventually join her. But there was no sign of him. She later found out, that he had been waiting at the dock with his friend and literary comrade, G. Venkatachalam, but ran off at the sight of the British police. Moments before the ship pulled up anchor, Venkatachalam rushed on board, greeted Ragini hurriedly, and handed her an illegible scrawl from Harin and some money before disappearing down the gangplank.

The seas had been stormy during the journey. Ragini was tired and unwell. She had kept secret, from both her husband and Harin, that she was expecting a child. Even in her eighth month her condition was barely noticeable; she carried herself well and the sari was a perfect cover. She had been reluctant to go through with this pregnancy, fearing it would interfere with her career. But just before leaving New York she had consulted a gypsy fortune-teller in Greenwich Village who predicted she would give birth to a baby girl who would grow up to become a dancer whose fame and career would surpass her own.

4

Kite Strings

Fearing a repetition of the reception she received in British-occupied Colombo, Ragini Devi tried to persuade the French captain of the S.S. *D'Amboise* to let her disembark in Pondicherry, a tiny enclave of France, just south of Madras. When he refused, she disclosed her condition and even threatened to kill herself. By this time she had worked herself into such a state of agitation that on the morning of 19 September 1930, before the ship reached Pondicherry, Ragini gave birth, a month prematurely, to a five-pound baby girl. Her daughter had long tapering fingers, big black eyes and an ancient look. Ragini had already chosen her name, "Indrani," Queen of Heaven, consort of Indra. She could picture the name in lights, blazing across the marquee.

The ship's doctor finally stepped in and took charge. Eager not to have his reputation sullied by the suicide of a hysterical woman, and anxious to avoid any further scandal on board ship, he demanded the captain and the French government authorities permit mother and child to disembark. The troublesome American and her baby were transported by stretcher directly to the hospital of the sleepy French provincial town. But even here, British detectives were on the alert. While Ragini lay frail and weak in her hospital bed, with limited funds and not knowing when she might be permitted to enter British India, her baggage was searched for subversive communist literature, and for clues to the whereabouts of Harin.

Explanations for his disappearance at the dock in Colombo trickled in circuitously. Apparently news of Harin absconding with a colleague's wife had hit the local scandal sheets in New York. Hoping to spread ugly rumours, and create mischief, someone in New York had mailed clippings of the story to all the Indian papers. Ragini was certain it was her husband. Nothing was published in the Indian press, but the gossip was picked up in Colombo. Following Ragini's departure, Harin, according to his friends, saw the story splashed across the papers in Colombo, lost his nerve, and got so drunk that he became unconscious and his heart almost stopped beating. These friends eventually urged Harin to return to India. He immediately rejoined the Civil Disobedience Movement and was picked up in Bombay a few days later, arrested and sentenced to a year in prison.

Ragini had no idea when she would see Harin again. Her funds were dwindling. Daily visits to the hospital by a young Indian, who introduced himself as a friend of Harin's wife, Kamala Devi, were her only source of comfort. On her release from the hospital, he arranged asylum for Ragini and her baby at a religious ashram where he resided. Unfortunately, the Aurobindo Ashram, as it was known, was run by a strong-willed, French-speaking Sephardic Jew, called "Mother," who discouraged Ragini from seeing much of this friend. "It would interfere with his yoga and his powers of concentration," she stated bluntly.

The real head of this spiritual retreat, Sri Aurobindo Ghosh, a philosopher, poet and patriot who withdrew to Pondicherry after a political trial, saw his disciples only twice a year. The "Mother" was his intermediary.

During Ragini's stay at the ashram, two sisters and a brother of

Harin's paid her a visit. They brought with them clothes for the baby and some money. That visit and subsequent help to Ragini was also initiated by Kamala Devi Chattopadhyaya, who was in jail, along with Harin and his older sister, Sarojini Naidu.

Motivated by her respect and admiration for Ragini the artist, and perhaps by her feminist ideology, this remarkable woman rose above any ill-feelings or jealousy, and from her prison cell directed her network of friends, relatives, colleagues and theosophists like Annie Besant, to assist Ragini and her baby in every possible way.

By the time Ragini got word directly from Harin she had given up on him. He sent her poems and wrote enthusiastically of starting their theatre work once he was out of jail. But Ragini began to have doubts; she was hurt at the way he had behaved. She heard rumours he was unreliable because of a drinking habit. Whenever he gave a performance or passed through an experience that demanded stamina, he would fall back on drink. All the great poets, she philosophised, were either highly immoral or drunkards, and sometimes both. One must expect them to be poets, not men. Harin's vast network of friends hoped jail would be a good discipline for him.

Ragini wrote in a letter back to a friend in New York that there were times she felt brokenhearted. But she was not out to reform anyone. Perhaps Harin was just a chance instrument in her life, perhaps they were destined to go their separate ways.

After about two months in the ashram, just when she was convinced she and her baby would perish in this backwater of France, Ragini was notified by the British consul that permission had been granted for her to enter India on a British passport. She immediately packed up her belongings, collected the baby, and took a night train across the border.

Waiting for her at the railway station in Madras was the same husky-voiced emissary who had delivered the note and money to her on board ship in Colombo. Venkatachalam, renowned art critic and a literary comrade and friend of Harin and his wife Kamala Devi, insisted Ragini and her daughter come to Bangalore as his guests. He explained he shared his home with Fred Harvey, a retired English businessman, pacifist, vegetarian, anti-vaccinationist and champion of Indian-made goods, who ran the Theosophical Centre situated on the premises.

Venkatachalam, in his writings, described the house on 6 St. John's Road as "a fairly well-known address in India . . . The birthplace of many social ideas and artistic activities, and a rendezvous for waifs and strays of the better sort, of both the East and the West." The neat, whitewashed bungalow in the Bangalore cantonment was nestled amidst sprawling grounds shaded by large tamarind trees and flowering jacaranda. Ragini and her baby were installed in a private room with an attached bath, overlooking a terrace, just off the central reception hall. And it was in this reception hall, some seventeen years later, that her daughter Indrani had her debut dance recital.

Ragini Devi was instantaneously swept into the daily life of 6 St. John's Road. The pleasant climate, peaceful surroundings, and nutritious vegetarian diet restored her spirits and health. She spent several hours each morning rehearsing and getting back into shape in the reception hall which was always at her disposal. In the evenings artists, writers and scholars collected in the cosy Theosophical Centre library to exchange ideas, argue politics, and inhale the sweet musky fumes of Fred Harvey's pipe. They were all intrigued by Ragini and eager to help her track down gurus of authentic Indian dance.

She was the only woman present when Venkatachalam took her along one evening to a performance of some dancing girls. The dance that caught her attention was the sprightly Kite Dance. "Patang"— the kite—she was told, represented the lover; the broken thread, a separation; and the recovery of the kite, a reunion. She expressed a desire to learn the dance and was told there was a retired palace dancer in Mysore who would teach her the dance properly. Arrangements were immediately made for her to travel to Mysore with her baby and study the dance from Jetti Tayamma—daughter of Dasappa, a famous palace wrestler from the time of Krishnaraja Wadiyar—who was reputed to be a legendary dancer of extraordinary talent, and one of the finest exponents of the Mysore school of Bharata Natyam.

Unlike Devadasis who served in the temples, and whose art was passed down from mother to daughter, Rajadasis auditioned for their appointment to the palace. And unlike temple dancers, who danced as part of ritual worship, palace dancers were attached to the royal courts to perform on special occasions like birthdays of Maharajas, the anniversary of coronations, and celebrations of the autumn Dussehra festival.

After teaching her the Kite Dance, Jetti Tayamma, a handsome, white-haired woman of about seventy, insisted that Ragini learn her signature piece as well: a dance set to a verse from the *Gita Govinda*, Jayadeva's epic poem, celebrating the love between Radha and Krishna.

The ageing dancer cleared her throat and began to sing *Yahi Madhava* in the soulful Raga Bhairavi. Diamond studs in her nostrils sparkled in the light of the oil lamps. Her graceful fingers, expressive eyes and every muscle of her face transformed Jetti Tayamma into the young, jealous, love-sick Radha, scolding her wayward lover Krishna:

"Having struggled through the night, she appeared withered by the arrow of love. She rebuked her lover as he touched her feet, pleading forgiveness . . .
Go Madhava! Go Krishna! Don't plead your deceitful words with me.
Go after her, she will dispel your anguish."

When the dance ended, no one spoke. The blowing of the sacred conch in the distance, echoing the eternal sound "Om," broke through the silence. Ragini Devi drew her green silk sari around her shoulders, leaned back against the wall, and closed her eyes. Pondicherry, Colombo, Marseilles, Paris, New York, Minneapolis, all dissolved into some past incarnation.

5

Veil of Illusion

agini Devi stepped into India's dance scene just as the anti-
nautch movement was gathering momentum and reaching a
crescendo. A missionary from London, known only as Miss
Tenant, who was the driving force behind the movement, had crusaded
zealously to abolish Indian dance. The "notorious nautch," performed
by dancing girls, was a typical after-dinner entertainment Indian
merchants provided for their customers from abroad. European men
were beguiled by the charm of the dance, but European ladies,
scandalised by the dancers' languishing glances and sultry smiles,
declared them wicked.

The Devadasis, socially ostracised by the British, had similarly
fallen into disrepute. Loss of royal patronage had forced some of
them into dubious professions. Their ancient art, rooted in the sacred
Vedas, was deemed immoral. A Devadasi bill, prohibiting the
employment of dancers in the temples, was proposed in the Madras

Assembly. Disdainful English puritans, as well as upper-class Hindus who had adopted Victorian attitudes, condemned indigenous artists, yet tolerated foreign ladies performing in public.

Occidental theatrical conventions—the proscenium stage, special lighting effects, beautifully crafted sets, and a price for admission—imbued public performances by foreign artists with a semblance of propriety and sophistication. The moral conduct of an individual artist was seldom in question. Ballet, symphony, opera, theatre and art exhibits, were essential components of "civilised" societies.

When Anna Pavlova toured India in the early twenties, her ballets were received with reverence. When Ruth St. Denis performed her interpretation of the nautch during her 1926–27 tour of India, she brought the house down with roars for an encore. Pavlova's early interest in traditional Indian dance coincided with the country's changing political climate: a growing surge of nationalism, bolstered by Mahatma Gandhi's efforts to emancipate women, had sparked in some Indians a renewed pride and awareness of their ancient heritage.

E. Krishna Iyer, an orthodox Brahmin advocate and freedom fighter, challenged opponents of dance by dressing in female Bharata Natyam costume and performing in public. His campaign to remove the stigma attached to dance further fuelled the battle between supporters of Miss Tenant and supporters of the pro-nautch movement.

Yet dance had not been entirely wiped out. A number of dedicated Devadasi families, believing it was their sacred duty, disregarded the ban on dance and continued to practise their art in secret.

Mylapore Gouri Amma, a retired Devadasi living in Madras, had, as a young woman, been the principal dancer at the Kapaliswaram temple. She agreed to take Ragini on as her pupil. A Bharata Natyam dancer of dignity, grace and expressiveness, Gouri Amma excelled in the art of abhinaya, and possessed a wealth of rare dances, taught to her by her mother. In the two months Ragini spent with her in 1931, Gouri Amma, with the help of her daughter who spoke a little English, passed down to Ragini the intricacies of expressive dance, gesture and music. Each gesture Gouri Amma imparted came with quotations from the *Natya Shastra*, with demonstrations and discourses on the subtle aspects of aesthetics connected to each minuscule glance.

By the time her training in Madras ended, Ragini, once again, found herself short on funds. Although Venka had arranged for her to stay with friends, there was still the tuition to pay, plus a small salary for the nanny she had hired to care for the baby. An invitation from a charitable organisation in Bangalore to participate in a performance of music and dance brought her back to the comfort and security of 6 St. John's Road.

Ragini was not properly prepared to perform since she was still without her costumes. It was a while before she discovered that Bajpai had taken possession of her costume trunk. Although she had contacted a lawyer in New York, claiming her husband had no right to her things, she had little hope of ever seeing the trunk again. With a small advance from the sponsors, she managed to have some new costumes hastily tailored in Bangalore. She pulled some of her New York repertoire out of mothballs, added the Kite Dance she had learned in Mysore, and began to practise daily. Musicians, both North Indian and South Indian, also participating in the programme, volunteered to accompany Ragini's dances. Since there was no printed schedule, she prefaced each dance with brief explanations of the themes and gestures in English. The audience and the press were charmed. Many were convinced she was "a high caste Hindu lady."

Spurred on by this enthusiastic reception, Ragini set off to conquer and to educate modern Indian audiences in other cities. She became her own impresario, stage manager, lighting designer and costume designer, and booked herself into the Royal Opera House in Bombay. The week's engagement drew glowing praise from the Indian audiences and received extensive press coverage. "The purity and precision which characterised the dances of Ragini Devi . . . ," wrote *The Times of India* critic, "reveal the reverence with which she approached her art, and the care with which she has mastered the symbolism of the ancient dance of India."

Her performances in Calcutta, a stronghold of puritans eager to banish the arts, had caused a stir. Would pure Bengali society tolerate a white dancing girl who had mastered the technique of Indian classical dance? Ragini believed they would. Calcutta was ripe for appreciation of her art. Genuine lovers of art had flocked to her performances at the Dalhousie Institute. Close to fifty respectable Hindu ladies, seated in the lower-priced seats, were exposed for the first time to the vast possibilities of the technique of classical Indian dance in a modern setting. Ragini's dances, one observer commented, gave expression to "a quiet enjoyment of healthy vigour and the joy of life—ingredients essential to the nation in its present stage of progress." "At the formative period of reconstruction in art," another observer commented, "the nation needed the assistance of those like Sri Ragini Devi who could give the degraded and decadent art of the dance, intellectual and social status."

O.C. Ganguly, renowned art critic, wrote in the *Amrita Bazaar Patrika*: "Our thanks are due to Ragini Devi, an enthusiastic lover of Indian art, and a skilful and accurate interpreter of classical Indian dancing for proving through demonstration that the great traditions of the old art of Indian dancing and dramatics are still living, foolishly neglected by modern exponents of so-called 'Oriental Dancing' and awaiting to be recognised, understood, learnt, and interpreted in its true and correct spirit, as a marvellously articulate and developed language of gestures, ready to hand, bequeathed to us in an unbroken sequence of development by generations of old masters and expert exponents from century to century."

For the next few years Ragini toured India from the Himalayas to Cape Comorin. She performed in theatres, movie houses, railway sheds, universities, and in grand palaces for nawabs, begums and maharajas. India's finest musicians, including Abdul Karim Khan and Bismillah Khan, often shared the stage with her. Ragini's entourage, in addition to her daughter, included four musicians, a variety of instruments, trunks bursting with costumes, and a Pathan bodyguard. Describing her arrival into Sholapur for a performance, she said: "My tonga led the procession, the bells on the horses jingling merrily. On the way we passed a brass band escorting a huge sign fixed on a bullock cart announcing the dance performance of Ragini Devi, world famous dancer. People stopped to stare at our cavalcade of musicians with red fezes, turbans, and musical instruments, and the baggage carts in charge of the Pathan, in his turban and pajamas. It was like a circus coming to town!"

Her repertoire included dances such as "Radha's Response," "The Bengal Vendor," "The Boat of Life" (set to Harin's "Boatman's Song") and "The Ecstatic Dance of Krishna," which invariably brought the house down.

In the early thirties, an invitation from the Maharaja of Travancore, to dance at the Arts Festival in Trivandrum, was to fulfil Ragini's long cherished dream to visit Kerala, home of Kathakali dance drama.

Following her own performance at the Travancore palace for a select audience of visiting dignitaries from England and their wives, Ragini had the opportunity to witness a full Kathakali dance drama staged in the palace gardens. After dinner, the beating of the chenda drums lured the visitors, and Ragini, outdoors. Chairs were placed for the Maharaja and his guests in front of a bright canvas canopy that had been set up against a backdrop of tall coconut palms. A solitary brass lamp-stand with a lighted wick burned in front of a rectangular curtain held up by two men with bare chests. A Malayalee gentleman, seated next to Ragini, explained that the velvet curtain, with its bands of black, green, red, gold and white represented the veil of illusion, Maya. The flickering flame was the presence of God. The dancers performed for this divine flame alone.

Obscured from the audience by the curtain, male dancers performed a ritual dance of invocation. Soon a pair of hands, with silver claws covering the fingers of one hand, gripped the curtain, gave it a vigorous shake and then vanished. The curtain was then lowered to reveal two superhuman characters in jewelled headdresses, their faces painted with fantastic green and red make-up and framed with moulded white borders. With a blood-curdling cry and shake of the shoulders they too vanished. The gradual unveiling of characters, the Malayalee gentleman whispered to Ragini, was a device to slowly transport mortals in the audience to the realm of the divine.

At the appearance of the sinister black demoness, Sarupanakha, dripping in fake blood, one English lady fainted in her chair and had to be carried away; by the time the play ended at dawn most of the English guests had departed and those who remained were Indian. Ragini recalled being "completely fascinated by the stylised movement and patterned gestures of the dance, so entirely different from any Indian dance I had seen."

Prior to her next engagement, which was in Trichur, Ragini wrote to the Kerala Kalamandalam, then situated in the nearby village of Uttukadu, informing them of her performance, and expressed her desire to visit the school. She was familiar with the story of how the school had been established by Kerala's great poet, Narayana Menon Vallathol. With funds raised by a local lottery, he crusaded to rescue Kathakali dance drama from obscurity and was slowly generating a revival of this art in Kerala. Her performance in Trichur was attended by Vallathol, his wife and several Kathakali gurus. The following morning, Mukunda Raja, the director of the Kerala Kalamandalam, and Vallathol's right-hand man, arranged for her to visit the centre and observe the dance classes.

The invocational dance prelude, Purappadu, was performed for her by a group of students clad only in white cotton loincloths. Guru Kunju Kurup, leading exponent of Kathakali, and his students performed for Ragini, without costume or make-up, an excerpt from a dance drama.

As she was leaving, Vallathol, who had become deaf and communicated mostly through Kathakali gestures, succumbed to Ragini's wishes and assured her she was welcome to return to Kalamandalam anytime to study both the male-dominated Kathakali and the feminine Mohini Attam. With this began the most formative years of Ragini's career, making her the first female, and the first foreigner to study Kathakali.

She returned to Kalamandalam soon after her touring commitments ended and with Indrani, who was three, in tow, moved into a small snake-infested cottage surrounded by tall areca palms, on the grounds of the school. There was no plumbing; the latrine, enclosed with palm fronds, was out in the fields behind the cottage. Meals were served on large banana leaves, on the veranda. They sat cross-legged on the floor and scooped up the spicy vegetarian food with their fingers. Each morning Ragini studied privately with Guru Kunju Kurup and with Ravunni Menon. She studied Mohini Attam with Kalyani Kutty Amma. An old man came daily to teach her the feminine roles, and each evening she joined the other students to practise eye movements and facial expressions. She shocked the local residents by having the ritual Kathakali massage which is given to male students for two weeks before sunrise during the monsoon season. After the body is rubbed with coconut oil, the student induces perspiration by dancing vigorously and performing gymnastics. He then lies on the ground, face down with the knees spread in a right angle, while the masseuse, holding on to a bar, massages the entire body with his feet, stimulating the nervous system and making the body beautifully supple.

Indrani, during this time, ran around barefoot and unbathed; a gang-leader of the boys and girls in the village, she climbed trees and carried a big stick in her hand to protect herself and her mother from strangers and from poisonous snakes. Her head was crawling with lice, and her fingers were infected with scabies. She devoured hot spicy dishes prepared for her by Vallathol's wife Amma, who loved her like a daughter, and she conversed in Malayalee, which she had picked up from the students, dancers and musicians. Gopinath, a handsome, young, superbly trained Kathakali dancer from Travancore, who was employed as a water-carrier at Kalamandalam, appointed himself Indrani's personal nursemaid. He doted on her like a mother hen. But he was also a stern disciplinarian and thought nothing of caning her with a thin green stick whenever the need arose.

A slender, swarthy youth, with sleek black hair down to his shoulders and vivid blazing eyes, Gopinath captured Ragini's attention right away. With the blessing of Vallathol and Mukunda Raja, he agreed to partner Ragini and join her on her tours, presenting abbreviated episodes from the Kathakali dance dramas. Mukunda Raja helped Ragini put together a fine group of musical accompanists led by vocalist Vishvanatha Bhagavatar, his son, Narayanaswamy, on the cymbals and Madhava Varyar, playing the maddalam.

While Ragini herself never tired of sitting through the traditional Kathakali dramas which lasted all night, for several days, she didn't believe it would find an audience outside Kerala, or even in the big cities of Kerala. In addition to presenting short excerpts she decided to modify the elaborate costume and make-up as well, so as to make the body movements and the facial expressions more visible. Initially there were raised eyebrows among die-hard Kathakali traditionalists. But they soon began to see wisdom in her vision. Kathakali, in its present form, had never prospered beyond the border of Kerala. In time, Ragini's interpretations of Kathakali, which she preceded with brief explanations in English, in theatres throughout Kerala and in cities across India, became instrumental in paving the way for traditional (though generally edited) Kathakali to become a vital part of the international dance scene.

From the Kathakali dance drama, Daksha Yagam, she adapted the romantic episodes of Shiva and Parvati to perform as a duet with Gopinath. While the dramatic text of the gesture songs and the choreography were in pure Kathakali tradition, the costumes and ornaments were drawn from bronze idols and sculpted figures of Shiva and Parvati; to make the Kathakali more accessible to the uninitiated, interspersed between these dances were items like the Hunter Dance, Peacock Dance and Garuda Dance—solos for Gopinath. Added to these were Ragini's solo Jathiswaram and tillana in the Bharata Natyam style, and her popular Kite Dance, Marwari Dance and Snake Dance, which once enticed a live cobra on to the stage!

In an article published some years later, Gopinath referred to his partnership with Ragini, stating: "The key to our success on the stage lay in the careful selection of scenes and in the artistic beauty and brevity of their presentation. May I record here that the entire credit for the successful presentation of the items went to Srimati Ragini Devi who organised the shows, decided on the costume and decor and generally guided me, and that my debt to her is boundless. I hope the lovers of Kathakali, and particularly the Kerala Kalamandalam, will remember the pioneering role played by her for making Kathakali known at a national and international level, at a time when the art was hardly respectable even on the soil of its own growth."

In 1934 Ragini and her troupe were invited by the poet Rabindranath Tagore to perform in Shantiniketan. One late-evening performance was interrupted by piercing cries which suddenly sprang from somewhere in the front row, making the cultured Bengali audience, seated under a languid starlit sky, almost jump out of their skins.

"What are you doing to my mother? What are you doing to my mother?" shrieked Ragini's four-year-old daughter, as she started to rush up on to the stage to rescue her mother from a ferocious demon who was chasing her around the floorboards.

Wearing the full traditional Kathakali make-up for a change, Gopinath was quite unrecognisable behind all the face paint and costume. A magnificent red moustache, outlined in white, curled up his cheeks, streaks of red rose above his eyebrows, then curved down his nose, his eyes were thickly outlined in black, knobs of white pith clung precariously on his forehead and on the tip of his nose, a jewel-studded headdress, bordered with iridescent green beetles' wings added three extra feet to his height, layer upon layer of bustling skirts added girth. Long silver claws on the fingers of his left hand shimmered in the light of oil lamps as he darted from one corner of the stage to the other, trying to grab an end of Ragini's sari and carry her off.

Indrani's hysteria subsided when the godlike Rabindranath Tagore, seated next to her, took her on his lap, stroked her head gently and calmed her down with soothing words. India's literary giant, Nobel laureate, painter, philosopher and founder of this open-air cultural institution, created near Calcutta in 1901, was delighted by the child's reaction. He turned around and explained to the agitated audience, in a voice that was surprisingly high-pitched for a man of his towering stature, that for a child the world of fantasy was real. The realm inhabited by gods and demons and angels and witches was real. The little girl's outburst had been natural and honest, as it should be.

Peace was restored in the audience and the performance continued. From the epic *Ramayana*, Sita Harana, the story of Sita's abduction by the demon-king, Ravana, was familiar to all Indians. The enactment of the episode in the Kathakali dance drama style from Kerala was, however, an entirely novel experience. There was little dancing in Sita Harana. The demon's amorous pursuit of Sita, his fury at her rejection of him and Sita's despair and terror were conveyed through expressive mime and gesture. Frantic drum beats heightened Sita's fears and Ravana's frenzied pursuit of her.

After the final performance, marking the close of a week's residency at Shantiniketan for the troupe, Tagore presented Ragini a handwritten note of gratitude, which he read out, expressing delight at the exhibition given by Ragini Devi. "Those of us belonging to Northern India," he said, "who have lost the memory of the pure Indian classical dance have experienced a thrill of delight." Tagore said he was grateful at the assurance it had brought to the audience that the ancient art was still a living tradition in India with its grace, vigour and subtleties of dramatic expression.

6

On the Road

For the next five years Ragini based her steadily expanding troupe in Bombay, where she enjoyed the patronage of a Sindhi businessman and admirer, Chandu Jagtiani. A handsome, soft-spoken gentleman, he relished his role as benefactor and patron of the arts.

A flat on the top floor of an office building in Ballard Estate was at their disposal, free of rent. The spacious dining room doubled as a dance studio and there, during breaks in their busy touring schedule, the troupe rehearsed, adding new items to their repertoire of dances and creating new costumes. They settled in like one great happy family, and took turns trying to tame Ragini's free-spirited daughter. The artists bathed her, combed and oiled her hair, cooked for her, fed her and were happy to let her sit in on the daily rehearsals. When Gopinath suggested Indrani dance the role of the golden deer, Maricha, the five-year-old was ecstatic and flung herself into the part with gusto. She had caught on at an early age that the only way to get sympathy, admiration and attention from her mother was to shine as a dancer.

She was unafraid on stage. Wrapped in gold lamé, she pranced across the floorboards, rolling her eyes from side to side, her fingers forming the face and antlers of a deer. In this episode from the *Ramayana*, Sita, unaware that Maricha is actually a demon in disguise, begs her husband to capture it. Rama obeys and chases after the deer, realising too late that it is Ravana's ploy to leave Sita unprotected in the forest. It was the prelude to the scene in Sita Harana that had sent Indrani screaming towards the stage that memorable evening in Shantiniketan.

Up to that time, no one had bothered with Indrani's schooling. She learnt to speak some English from her mother, Malayalee from the dancers and musicians but, besides the role of the golden deer, little else. Jagtiani suggested to Ragini that she place her daughter in a Catholic convent, located in suburban Bandra, that had a fine reputation. At the boarding school, Indrani would be taught how to read and write, speak proper English, use a knife and fork, and lead a more orderly, disciplined life. At the convent, Indrani brooded and wept for most of the week and came to life only on the weekends, when members of the troupe would come to visit. The nuns in charge of the largely English boarding school did little to stop other students from calling her a "fatherless half-breed heathen," and the Mother Superior, to shield the savage from Satan's clutches, placed a picture of Saint Joseph over her bed. As a double precaution, she persuaded her to memorise The Lord's Prayer and recite it several times a day.

During this time, new political reforms and a brief lull in British antagonism towards the Indian National Congress presented an opportunity for Ragini's long-vanquished husband to return to his homeland.

Ramlal Bajpai, aware that his former colleague Harin Chattopadhyaya was no longer in the picture, came filled with hopes and expectations of a reconciliation with his wife. In addition, a relation back in Nagpur had made a lucrative job offer. But by the time he arrived in India, another enterprising relation had appropriated the job for himself.

He received an icy reception from Ragini who was absorbed in her rehearsals and performances and would have nothing to do with him. Disillusioned by India, and finally able to accept the fact that dance, for Ragini, would always come before anything or anyone else, he cut his visit short and returned to America earlier than planned.

Before he left, Ragini, however, consented to one of his requests— to stop by the convent and meet with Indrani. She alerted her daughter that the stranger who might be taking her out for the day was her "Uncle Ram." Indrani was thrilled to discover she at least had an uncle. Whenever she had quizzed Ragini about her father, all her mother would say was that he had been a high-class Brahmin who had died before she was born. Indrani and her "Uncle" spent the afternoon strolling along Juhu Beach, munching bhel puri, and getting acquainted. Before he dropped her back at the convent, he took her shopping to Crawford market and bought her a pair of smart patent leather shoes that she had her eye on.

Ragini was on the move as well. More than eight years in India were drawing to a close. After months and months of negotiations, and with money borrowed from Jagtiani, she embarked on what was planned as a three-month tour of Europe.

Their tour kicked off to a perfect start. The introduction of Kathakali to audiences in Paris caused a sensation. The curator of the Museum of Oriental Art, Janine Auboyer, declared that "the Muse Guimet had been infused to life by Ragini Devi's recital."

At London's Arts Theatre Club, Ragini staged "Mohini Bhasmasura," a dance drama portraying the struggle between good and evil. In the words of the Indian writer, Mulk Raj Anand, who was at this performance:

"Ragini and Gopinath performed the ballet, choreographed by Ragini Devi, with consummate skill. She showed the cruelty in the heart of a force of nature unschooled by the spirit, ultimately resolving the crisis of the power maniac who destroys himself. Ragini seemed to me to have introduced into Bhasmasura all the primitivism of wild nature. The audience on that evening applauded as though it had become the chorus, absorbing the truth of the struggle between beauty and terror, in the world of poetry which came into the theatre. The confrontation through the symbolic gesture language of Kathakali had cut out all decorative asides, posing truth against unbridled urges in a magnificent metamorphosis of moods through perceptions . . ."

According to Anand, the German choreographer and dancer Kurt Jooss—who also explored the struggles between good and evil in his famous 1932 ballet, *The Green Table,* an expressionistic view of the origins of war—was deeply moved by Ragini's presentation and came to every single performance.

Battles between good and evil, explored in the ballets of both Jooss and Ragini, were on the brink of spilling onto the world stage. The bulk of Ragini's European engagements included a month-long tour of Germany, capped off by a command performance for Adolf Hitler. But at the last moment the dance troupe was refused visas. It was 1939. German Panzer tanks were rolling into Poland. Europe was at war. The performances were cancelled.

Ragini was stranded in Paris with twelve artists to feed, house and care for, and money was rapidly evaporating. She ran up a substantial bill at a small neighbourhood café and owed the hotel over a month's rent.

One of the North Indian musicians, who had not been with the troupe as long as the others, became hysterical. He managed to collect the passports of the other performers and reported Ragini's state of affairs to the British High Commission, under whose jurisdiction they fell. The high commission ordered the immediate return of the members of the troupe to India. Ragini, who had held onto her passport, had other plans for herself and her daughter.

Indrani watched in disbelief as the procession of dancers and musicians, her family for the last several years, trooped out of their dismal Paris hotel. The three Kathakali dancers and seven musicians, dressed in borrowed, ill-fitting wool suits, dragged their drums, trunks and bundles down three flights of stairs. At intervals, the minute-light would switch off, plunging them into a darkness that mirrored their mood. Gopinath, who the precocious and worldly-wise Indrani suspected was Ragini's current lover, and some other artists were sobbing openly. This premature end to their grand tour of Europe was hardly what they had anticipated. So long as Ragini had been under official sponsorship of the Muse Guimet, the concierge of the small residential hotel had remained patient and civil. But the sight of guests trooping out en masse, baggage and all, was another matter.

The usually genial landlady began to leave notes for Ragini, demanding immediate settlement of the bills. Ragini avoided direct confrontation with her by entering and exiting the hotel by a back door. Ultimately the concierge, who had befriended Indrani, fed her cups of free hot chocolate, and even allowed her to keep a kitten in the room, cornered the child. "You go find your mother," she said, vigorously shaking a finger in the girl's face. "If she doesn't pay up her bills at once, I call the police."

In the meantime, Ragini began to pack her bags and arranged for a van and driver to come to the back door of the hotel. Late at night, while police pounded on the front door, costume trunks, suitcases and instruments, including a giraffe-like tanpura packed in a box resembling a coffin, were quietly hauled out the window into the van. Indrani wanted to take her kitten along. There was no time, Ragini explained. The police were about to break the door open. They would retrieve the animal later.

The van, driven by a young French stagehand willing to die for Ragini, sped them directly to the Gare du Nord. There the driver loaded mother, daughter, coffin and all, into the first available boat-train to London.

Aided by friends, Ragini found a damp, cheerless basement flat in central London, within walking distance of a London County school, where she immediately enrolled Indrani. While Londoners nervously scanned the skies for German bombs and ran around carrying gas masks, Ragini dashed about the city renewing contacts from her earlier visit. She approached the India Society of London and negotiated solo performances. Indians residing in London, including the eminent Indian musicologist, Narayana Menon, pitched in and provided musical accompaniment. Ragini put her daughter to work as well and Indrani joined her on stage for some of the performances.

It took little coaxing; she was stage-struck, and ever since her debut as the golden deer, easily intoxicated by the sound of applause.

Ragini presented an artistically successful series of performances and lecture demonstrations at the University of London, at Oxford University, and at Dartington Hall. She was admired and respected and received flattering reviews, and was, on several occasions, wined and dined by upper crust London society, yet the money coming in was barely sufficient to survive on.

A note once arrived by messenger from Winston Churchill's daughter, Lady Sarah Churchill, inviting Ragini and Indrani to her home for afternoon tea. Her ulterior motive, it turned out, was to paint a portrait in oil of Indrani dressed in Indian peasant costume. Lady Churchill was so fascinated by the exotic pair she invited them back for a formal dinner.

It was a very grand affair, replete with ladies in long gowns, weighted under diamond tiaras, and gentlemen in black tie and tails, seated under crystal chandeliers at a very long table set with fine china, crystal goblets, bowls of fresh roses, and gleaming silver candelabras with serpentine claws. An army of stone-faced butlers, in white gloves, silently dished out mountains of rare delicacies. Ragini, looking radiantly beautiful in a Banaras silk sari and jewels pulled out of her costume trunk, gobbled up everything so fast she choked on an oyster. The gentleman seated next to her jumped up and gave her a swift thump on the back. She spat the oyster out on her plate, smiled apologetically, and then went right back to shovelling in the food.

Her daughter turned crimson with shame.

"You make me sick, Ragini," she hissed when she found a moment alone with her mother. "Are all you Americans brought up with such disgusting manners?"

Before they had set off from India, Ragini had asked her daughter to address her as Ragini and not mother. It would ruin her stage image, she felt, if people thought she was married and had a family.

Ultimately the day-to-day struggle to make ends meet in war-ravaged London forced Ragini to consider returning to America. She was unprepared for the complications this seemingly simple decision presented. Through her marriage to an Asian, Ragini had forfeited her American citizenship. She was now a British subject with a British passport and was denied a visa. Ragini turned to her family in Minneapolis for help, and in due course received an official certificate of birth. This seemed acceptable to the American embassy in London, but they continued to deny her daughter, who was included in her passport, permission to enter America.

A neighbour who lived in the flat above suggested to Ragini that she try entering America through Canada instead. The country was a member of the British Commonwealth so no visas or entry permits would be required. The neighbour happened to be Canadian and had some useful connections. In exchange for her typewriter, camera, a few other valuables, and whatever cash she could scrape up, he offered to make the necessary travel arrangements.

Some weeks later mother and daughter were received in Toronto by their neighbour's aunt and uncle. After a day's rest in a comfortable suburban home, Ragini and her daughter were driven to Niagara Falls. Canadians, it seems, regularly crossed the American border near Niagara Falls to do their laundry. To avoid attracting attention, Ragini had replaced her customary sari with a Western style dress and washed the exotic make-up off her face. Just before they reached the border, Indrani, who was nine at the time and quite tall for her age, was stuffed into a large laundry bag and ordered to curl up and lie quietly in the back seat of the car.

They slipped through customs and immigration and into the United States without incident, then proceeded on to Minneapolis on their own, uncertain of the welcome awaiting them.

7

Spring Festival Dance

The walls of the warm wood-panelled parlour of the Shermans' Minneapolis home were plastered with photographs Ragini had sent them from her years in India. There were ornately framed pictures of Ragini posing in a sari in front of the Taj Mahal, pictures of Ragini riding an elephant, a colour-tinted snapshot of her sprawled languorously on an Oriental carpet, another one of Ragini twirling about in a flared gypsy skirt, her midriff daringly bare. Alongside were pictures of Indrani perched on top of a carved Kashmiri rosewood table, and one of her crouching in a bucket full of water in Shantiniketan. Alex and Ida Sherman had long relinquished any hope of seeing their daughter again. When Ragini first ran off to India, without a word to anyone or even a goodbye, they had been mystified. Anonymous letters, supposedly mailed to them by Ramlal Bajpai, contained lurid accounts of Ragini's flight to India with a penniless, communist reprobate poet. Ida Sherman gave in to hysterics and lay sick in bed for a month. But Ragini had indicated no hints of any great disaster to her parents or asked for money, so they comforted themselves into believing some demented soul had fabricated most of the stories.

Now Ida was content to have her daughter and granddaughter home. She spent endless hours in the kitchen baking cakes and apple pies, and concocting recipes for her finicky, vegetarian offspring. She filled the house with fresh flowers and pampered her granddaughter with luxurious hot baths in the tub. Her immediate mission was to tame the little savage from India with "that unpronounceable name." She objected to her granddaughter staying out in the sun too long and worried her complexion would get darker. She curled the girl's long brown hair with strips of old newspapers she had been saving for the neighbourhood war effort. She pulled out patterns and ran up a closetful of dresses for her on the sewing machine. Alex Sherman was more openly perplexed over his grandchild's ethnicity. "What is your race, your nationality?" he demanded to know. "Are you a Caucasian or are you an Asian or what are you?"

"Ragini tells me my father was Indo-Aryan, a Brahmin, so I guess that's what I am." "But you can't be an Aryan, I'm an Aryan, a German Aryan," he argued. "Well, if you're also an Aryan, then I must be a double Aryan," she shot back. Sherman, amused by her quick retort, rewarded her by agreeing to subscribe to the newspaper with the funny papers that she had been begging for.

After some weeks of readjusting to American family life, Ragini escorted her now sartorially splendid daughter off to the local grammar school. She registered her as "Rani Sherman." Place of birth: Corsica. This Corsican "Ronnie" quickly began to make friends with people her own age.

Indrani developed a close bond with her grandparents, and was just settling in to the comfort, routine and stability of her new life when Ragini suddenly announced they were packing their trunks and moving to New York. The Shermans pleaded with her not to drag the child along, to let her at least complete her schooling and be raised in a civilised manner. But it was not an option Ragini would consider even for a moment. A few months of Minneapolis was more than she could endure, she announced to her daughter as they prepared to leave. She'd had enough apple pie and dumplings. She would perish and die if she didn't get back on stage right away.

Ragini Devi brought to New York a knowledge of Indian classical dance envied by other "ethnic" dancers. Oriental dance styles, popularised by Denishawn, La Meri, Jack Cole, the Kraft Sisters and others, were quite the rage. Setting Indian dance to fast-paced American rhythms was gaining popularity. Raymond Scott's "Dinner Music for a Pack of Hungry Cannibals" and Gene Krupa's rapid-fire drumming in "The Big Noise from Winnetka" had spiced up exacting, expressionless versions of Bharata Natyam movements. Now dancers were hungry for the real thing. La Meri, the all-American Texan with a wonderful sense of humour, was frank enough to admit she would "give her eyeteeth to know what Ragini Devi knew about Indian dance and music."

Ragini's total "Indianness" and "Hinduness" set her apart from the local dancers. Ruth St. Denis, who had settled comfortably into her role as the First Lady of American Dance, invited Ragini to teach at her school. But Ragini preferred to remain her own boss. She rented a studio in Carnegie Hall and set up The Indian Dance Theatre which in a short time began to attract lovers of India and Indian dance. Many who had studied with Ruth St. Denis and La Meri came to expand their vocabulary. Ragini renewed her earlier ties and contacts and launched into conducting classes in Bharata Natyam and Kathakali, lecturing at Columbia University, and performing. She trained a small group of dancers and began to tour across the country with them.

According to Litia Namoura, one of her leading dancers, Ragini's life was one constant struggle, an arduous life with all creativity done on a shoestring. She choreographed new dances, dyed materials, sewed her own costumes, put together the music, designed the lighting, produced her own performances and managed all her own publicity.

But a rift was growing between her daughter and herself. Since the escape from Paris, there was friction between them. While she loved dancing with Ragini's troupe and going on tour, Indrani had lost trust in her mother.

Little annoyances began to pile up. One time she asked her mother to buy her a pair of shoes she had seen displayed in a shop window. "The next time I have some money," Ragini promised. But when she next had money to spare, it was invested in a dinner at a Chinese restaurant.

Despite the discord, Indrani thrived on all New York had to offer and set out to make the most of it. Ragini had enrolled her in a children's theatre group in a midtown church where she participated in the annual Nativity plays. She played the role of Ophelia in a production of *Hamlet*, and in one of her earliest reviews, dancing with Ragini, she was singled out in *The Herald Tribune* for her role as the golden deer. At the Julia Richman High School, that she attended in Manhattan, she fell in with a gang of star-struck teenagers whose major preoccupation was chasing celebrities. They cut school to prowl midtown hotels: The Gotham, The Sherry Netherlands, The Plaza. They kept vigil by the stage door of Carnegie Hall and bagged autographs from the likes of Louis B. Mayer, Humphrey Bogart, Lauren Bacall and Frank Sinatra.

When Rita Hayworth was in town, the girls tracked her down at her suite at the Waldorf Astoria. A maid who answered the door tried to chase them away and began shouting for security guards. Just then the actress poked her head out to see what all the commotion was about, and much to the maid's chagrin, obligingly signed her name in all their autograph books. When she asked the girls their names they flew into hysterics and fled down the corridor before security guards could grab them and hand them over to the truant officer. Indrani, one of the main instigators of the Rita Hayworth expedition, got so worked up she lost control of her bladder and left a watery trail all the way to the front entrance of the hotel.

This little embarrassment didn't deter her from feeling superior to her classmates. She felt the schools she attended in Minneapolis and New York were far inferior to the British schools she had briefly attended in Bombay and London. She enjoyed subjects like literature, English and history, but was much happier when she was rehearsing and touring with Ragini's troupe.

Ragini, meanwhile, was interminably concocting schemes to

augment her meagre dance income and come up with each month's rent for the dance studio and for their small walk-up apartment on East 64th Street. In one of her more outrageous schemes she stepped perilously close to the wheels of a speeding cab with the idea of staging an accident, and then suing the driver for personal injury. Fortunately a last-minute surge of rationality held her back.

One Pandit Acharya, an enterprising Bengali freedom fighter, who had entered America posing as a dancer in Ruth St. Denis' company managed to get Ragini a part-time job at a midtown ladies' exercise salon where he periodically taught classes in yoga. There Ragini perfected the art of fabricating flattering measurements on matronly waistlines and was soon in great demand as an instructor.

Acharya had himself elevated flattery to an art form. The few dollars he had saved he invested in a large supply of ordinary cold cream. Then, clad in a bright saffron turban and gold hoop earrings, he convinced a leading Manhattan department store to let him set up a counter for his special "Camels' Milk Cold Cream," guaranteed to permanently remove all wrinkles.

Ladies, hypnotised by the wily dark-skinned swami's penetrating gaze, came in droves to buy his cream and have him smear their hands and faces with his magical potion. Those same ladies, plus the ladies from the exercise salon, also flocked to study yoga and feast on vegetarian food at his ashram in Nyack-on-the-Hudson which he had established with money amassed from the Camels' Milk Cold Cream.

The moment Ragini returned to New York, Ramlal Bajpai fled the city and moved to Washington D.C. New York, he complained to his friends, had grown much too small for the two of them. In Washington he had found a job translating Hindi for the War Office. He was able to continue his revolutionary activities as well since the city was crawling with anti-British spies who regularly briefed him on all recent developments pertaining to the Independence Movement.

Ragini looked up friends they used to have in common and renewed her old connections. The network of Indian expatriates, Indian visitors championing support for freedom, and Indians married to Americans, spread across the city and beyond. In reconnecting with the old crowd she also stoked up rumours from the past. People remembered, only too well, the scandal caused by Ragini's escapade to India with Harin. Tongues began to wag. Who was Indrani's father? Ramlal Bajpai or Harin Chattopadhyaya?

A popular gathering place for Indians in Manhattan was the East 10th Street apartment of Haji Hanif Abdul Razzack and his American wife, Elly—close friends of Harin and Kamala Devi. Indian students visiting from Washington, Philadelphia and Boston often ended up there. A regular visitor to their home was Jawaharlal Nehru's sister, Mrs. Vijayalakshmi Pandit, who stayed there with her three young daughters whenever she was in town. She had travelled to America to protest the credentials of the British-Indian delegation attending the United Nations Conference in San Francisco, believing they were British stooges who did not represent India. Indian freedom fighters rallied round her, but she was still struggling to convince the American government.

To help celebrate her daughter Lekha's twenty-first birthday, Mrs. Pandit invited a group of friends to the Razzack apartment for dinner. Indrani, who had just turned fourteen and was invited as a last-minute replacement for a female guest who had dropped out, went along with Ragini to the festivities. It was her first grown-up evening out in New York; she spent the entire day in preparation and dressed with great care in the finest dress she owned.

Milling about the living room of the spacious Greenwich Village apartment was an eclectic collection of Indians, Americans and Indo-Americans, conversing excitedly, sipping cocktails and munching on snacks. Ragini began almost immediately to scour the room for potential dancers and musicians. She enjoyed nothing more than a lively party, but this particular evening her mind was mostly preoccupied with the new ballet, based on Tagore's Spring Cycle Poems, that she was currently choreographing.

Indrani, from the moment she walked in, could feel people staring at her. She realised at once she was not the only person in the room under such keen scrutiny. Heads were turning between her and a stocky young man who was standing by a window smoking a cigarette; she could hear people around her whispering. It sank in for the first time that Ragini had perhaps lied to her about her father being dead.

It turned out that the young man by the window was Harin and Kamala Devi's only son, Rama Chattopadhyaya, who was visiting from Boston. Ragini laughed off Indrani's demands to know if there was any truth to the rumours and speculation circulating as to their relationship, and before dessert could be served Ragini had managed to recruit Rama Chattopadhyaya into playing the tabla for her next performance.

Indrani remained pensive all evening as the adults dissected India's political future with Syed Hussain, a spokesman for the Indian nationalist cause. In addition to being Mrs. Pandit's political supporter, he was rumoured to be the secret love of her life. There was talk of the British actually quitting India, there was talk of Muslims threatening to partition India, talk of a possible blood bath. In a room filled with Hindus and Muslims who were getting along famously, the idea seemed absurd. Mrs. Pandit, a Hindu, sat contentedly by the Muslim Syed Hussain's feet, one arm resting possessively over his knees.

Indrani's gaze wandered restlessly about the room and finally settled on the friend Rama Chattopadhyaya had brought along to the party. Rama's roommate from Boston was a handsome 29-year-old Bengali Muslim from Calcutta, who had graduated from MIT with a master's degree in both architecture and engineering.

Indrani studied the dark-skinned man with his long, wavy black hair. Ragini's casting problems, she thought excitedly, were solved. The Bengali would make an ideal God of Spring in Ragini's new ballet.

Two days later the architect turned up to audition for Ragini at the Carnegie Hall studio. He came armed with a curved cardboard sword covered in gold foil, and an Arab drummer named Yosuf in tow. When Ragini asked to see what he could dance, he flung off his shirt and shoes, and leaped about swinging his sword from side to side, while Yosuf pounded on the dholak.

He was hired for the role, and the "Sabre Dance" was added to the Indian Dance Theatre repertoire.

While he was ideally suited for the role, Ragini found his name, Habib Rahman, unsuitable for the stage and changed it in the programme to the more Hindu-sounding "Ritu Raj," prince of spring.

The role of the God of Spring demanded little dancing. Ritu Raj for the most part simply stood centre stage, looking very handsome in a gold dhoti, while pretty little spring flowers, led by Indrani, danced around him. He balanced on one foot, and waved his arms about like the famous Indian dancer, Uday Shankar, and received rave reviews.

Some weeks after the premiere performance of the Spring Festival Dance at the New York Times Hall, Ragini, Indrani, Habib and others were invited by Razzack and Elly to attend a performance of *Tristan and Isolde* at the Metropolitan Opera. This was Indrani's first evening at the opera. She traded her adolescent skirt and bobbysocks for one of her mother's silk saris and instantly appeared all grown-up and luminously beautiful. In the darkened theatre, overcome by the sadness of the sublimely beautiful *Liebestod* aria, she reached out and clutched the hand of the God of Spring seated next to her.

The couple's romance blossomed on stage. Habib left Boston, where he had been working for Walter Gropius, Lawrence Anderson, and other area architects, and moved to New York. Besides moonlighting as a dancer in Ragini's troupe, he was hired to work for the architect Ely Kahn.

After rehearsal one evening he walked Indrani over to the Ceylon India Inn, where Indians often congregated, for a meal.

A group of Indian men, apparently connected to the Bombay film world, were seated at a nearby table. They were laughing and conversing loudly and drinking beer. One of the men stood up and staggered over to Indrani.

"We have taken a bet, madam," he said, breathing beer into her face. "I say your father is Ramlal Bajpai. That gentleman says your father is Harin Chattopadhyaya. What do you say?"

His companions laughed and cheered him on. Indrani, at a rare loss for words, ran out of the restaurant and down West 44th street. She felt humiliated. She didn't have an answer.

Habib was equally upset and realised it was critical for Indrani's

Esther aged 3 & DeWitt aged 1½ years

*Esther Sherman, graduation
from West High*

*Ida Sherman, Esther
& Alexander Otto Sherman*

Esther in silent films

Esther, aka *Rita Cassilas, (above left & below) c. 1918 (above right) c. 1920*

Esther, wedding photo, c. 1920

Ramlal Bajpai & Esther/Ragini Devi, New York, 1930

Ragini Devi & Ramlal Bajpai, New York, early 1920s

Ragini Devi, Bangalore, India, 1933

Gopinath & Ragini Devi (in Sita Harana)*, India, 1933*

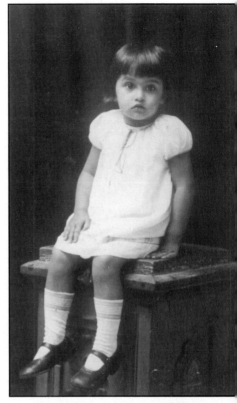

Indrani in Shantiniketan

Indrani, Bangalore, 1933
Photo: Venkatachalam

Habib Rahman aka Ritu Raj
& Indrani, backstage,
New York, 1945

Indrani, aged 14, New York
Photo: Ethel Preiss

Habib Rahman as Ritu Raj, New York, 1945

Ragini, Habib, Indrani, New York, 1946

Indrani, New York, 1945
Photo: Henry Kent

Wedding of Habib and Indrani. Seen with John Haynes Holmes,
New York, 11 May 1946

Ragini Devi as Kali, 1946 (reaction to daughter's wedding)

(Left) Habib & Indrani honeymooning in Asbury Park, New Jersey

(Below) Sukanya & Ayah, Chand Banu Bibi, Calcutta, 1950

(Above)
Rahman family,
Calcutta, 1947

(Right) Indrani in
Bharata Natyam,
Calcutta, 1950
Photo: Habib Rahman

Miss India contest, Bombay, 1952
Nargis, Indrani, Raj Kapoor, S.K. Patil

Sukanya & Indrani, 1952

self-esteem, and sense of identity to be told the truth about her father. He suggested they confront Ragini together. She stuck to her original story of the father being dead, but finally, under mounting pressure, she capitulated and confessed that "Uncle Ram" was not really an uncle, but Indrani's natural father.

But speculation, mostly on the part of Harin Chattopadhyaya, floated about for several years. The matter wasn't laid to rest until many years later when Harin met up with Indrani in Madras. He admitted rather shyly that he had very much hoped she would turn out to be his daughter. But the beautiful, shapely woman, seated before him at the Elphinstone Ice Cream Parlour, had Bajpai's wide-set eyes, high cheekbones and generous mouth. The resemblance was unmistakable.

Indrani's reunion in Washington with her newly discovered father occurred earlier than anticipated and under somewhat delicate circumstances.

When Habib Rahman formally asked Ragini for her daughter's hand in marriage, she had thrown a fit.

"And what's to become of me?" she fumed.

She threw him out of her troupe and forbade him to see her daughter again. The idea that Indrani could even consider abandoning her, or the dance troupe, stunned her. In her rage she struck her daughter with a chair and locked her up in their small apartment. Indrani escaped out a window, climbed down the fire escape and ran to the nearest subway. She asked some stranger for a subway token and eventually found her way to the apartment of an Indian couple, old friends of both Ragini Devi and Ramlal Bajpai, and begged for protection.

But Ragini soon tracked her down. She phoned the Marathes and threatened to call the police.

"Yes, Ragini Devi," challenged the ordinarily docile Mrs. Marathe before slamming the phone down. "Do call the police so I can tell them a thing or two about you!"

The Marathes admitted they had long suspected the true identity of Indrani's father. They encouraged her to meet and talk with Bajpai in Washington and get his advice and blessings.

Indrani went to Washington by train but found little sympathy there. "Uncle Ram" was not willing to sanction this marriage either. He had only just begun to feel like a real father. He was not about to give his daughter away so hastily. Besides, fifteen was too early for marriage, especially to a man who was sixteen years her senior. What was worse was that he was a Muslim.

Coincidentally, Bajpai's prime source of information in Washington happened to be Habib's older brother, Obaidur, who was press attaché in British India's high commission there. The fact that Obaidur was a friend and fellow nationalist made little difference. "Stay with me in Washington," Bajpai pleaded with his daughter. "Finish high school. I'll send you to college, you can study law, or medicine. But please don't become an artist like that Ragini Devi."

Indrani returned to New York with nothing resolved. The situation seemed hopeless. She was fifteen and expecting a child. Maximilian, an urbane European friend of Habib's, suggested the most practical solution would be for her to terminate the pregnancy, and arranged for her to meet with two sisters who agreed to perform an abortion. But at the last minute she lost her nerve; the sight of the two sinister-looking ladies wearing identical black dresses scared her off; besides she had never in her life visited a doctor, leave alone had an operation of any kind.

She was in a rush to get married and escape from her mother. She longed to return to India, and to the artists who had raised her and cared for her. More than that she was resolute in her ambition to have a great career as a dancer. Habib had his ambitions as well and envisioned erecting grand monuments and designing modern low-cost housing in India. Neither of them believed any conflict would erupt between Hindus and Muslims in India.

Habib tried once again to get Ragini to change her mind, but she remained violently opposed to the match. As a last resort, he stooped to bribery. If she would lie about her daughter's age and consent to the marriage, he would pay the passage for Ragini to eventually join them in India.

My parents were married at the Community Church of New York on 11 May 1946. The Reverend John Haynes Holmes, champion of

India's freedom struggle, and Mahatma Gandhi's American Apostle, performed the simple, civil ceremony. It was attended by Ragini, a few close friends, and myself, comfortably nestled in the womb under my mother's new yellow linen dress.

8

Panch Number

From the outset, my parent's return to India had been riddled with obstacles. When, after a brief honeymoon in Asbury Park, New Jersey, the newlyweds had tried to book a passage to India, they were in for a surprise—no one would issue them a ticket. It seemed Ragini Devi, convinced her son-in-law would not stick to his part of their bargain and would forget all about sending for her once he was settled in India, had alerted all the shipping lines in New York that her daughter, who was a minor, might try to leave the country. She threatened to file a suit against any company that would sell Indrani a ticket. Eventually, after numerous failed attempts, a sympathetic young woman at the American President Lines office, suggested it might be conceivable for the couple to sail quietly out of San Francisco instead.

Habib's brother in Washington, who had advanced him money for the passages, had also managed to obtain a British Indian passport for Indrani. Dealing with immigration was yet another problem. "Where and when did you enter the country?" they wanted to know. They had no record of Indrani's arrival in America. "What was your maiden name? What was your port of entry?" She had been a child, she said. She could remember nothing. The immigration officer spread out a map of the country and tried to jog her memory. Indrani pointed towards Niagara Falls, momentarily reliving the humiliating journey in the laundry bag. The man stamped some papers: port of entry, Buffalo, New York.

Just before they sailed off they informed Ragini of their plans by telegram and assured her they would send for her once they were adequately settled in India. At last the young couple pulled away from the shores of America on the tenth of July. The towers of the Golden Gate Bridge, partially obscured by fog, were their last glimpse of the country they had both called home for almost six years.

The first indications of trouble crackled over the radio of the *S.S. General Gordon* as the ship was approaching Bombay Harbour. Mohammed Ali Jinnah, leader of the Muslim League, had declared 16 August 1946 "Direct Action Day." His mission was to prove to the British, and to the Hindus, that India's Muslims were prepared to form a separate Islamic nation, Pakistan, even if it meant civil war.

In Calcutta, Shaheed Suhrawardy, unscrupulous, self-appointed leader of the Bengali Muslims, declared a public holiday. Police were conspicuously absent as he led his ruffians on a killing spree. With blood-curdling cries they ran through the streets of the city butchering Hindus with knives, axes, lathis, flaming torches—anything they could lay their hands on. Hindus retaliated with equal ferocity. As soon as my parents stepped ashore in Bombay they tried contacting my father's family in Calcutta, but it was impossible to get through. There was no way of knowing if they were dead or alive. Despite my father's fears and hesitations, my mother had her mind set on continuing directly to Calcutta. Plans for my father to spend some weeks job-hunting in Bombay were dropped.

The train to Calcutta, carrying the Muslim and his half-Hindu bride, arrived almost empty, while on the other side of the platform millions of refugees, carting their wretched little bundles, were crowding into trains headed out of Howrah Station. Taxi-stands stood empty. The few palki-gari wallahs, lined up outside the station, refused to drive the oddly matched pair to their destination. After lengthy negotiations, and at an outrageous price, a Muslim driver reluctantly tied the steamer trunks to the top of the carriage and whipped his half-starved nag on through the deserted streets.

The shutters of the once elegant carriage were shut tight. It made little difference. What she could see, peering through the slats, made the young bride's stomach turn over. She froze in terror and silently cursed herself for having been so stubborn about rushing to Calcutta.

Vultures circling the monsoon-darkened skies were the only visible signs of life. Hacked and mutilated corpses rotting alongside the road gave off a vile stench. The carriage clattered ominously on through the wide open spaces of colonial Calcutta, a hodgepodge of Victorian-Moghul, neo-Gothic, pseudo-Greek, and imitation-French Renaissance architecture. It clattered past more corpses lying in a marble fountain decorated with naked ladies. As the palki-gari turned into Park Circus, a predominantly Muslim locality, burnt and gutted houses came into view. Abandoned lorries were stacked with dead bodies. Flies, vultures and dogs feasted on corpses lying in large municipal garbage bins. The driver brought the carriage to a halt in front of the locked wrought-iron gate of 5 Pearl Road. The air reeked of petrol, but "Panch Number," the family home, appeared to be unharmed. Dr. Ghani, Habib's brother-in-law (Dulha Bhai) had, just at that moment, stepped out to hang a towel to dry over the second-floor veranda. "Babu! Babu! Babu!" he started to cry as soon as he spotted the two steamer trunks tied to the top of the carriage that had stopped in front of the house.

The foreign-returned bridegroom, and his bride, dazed and nauseous, were instantly engulfed by parents, brothers, sisters, nieces, nephews, uncles, aunts. They were all at once embracing and kissing and touching feet and sobbing out stories of recent horrors. Even though it was a Muslim neighbourhood, the house next door to Panch Number was owned and occupied by a Hindu family. When the killings erupted, Habib's family disguised their Hindu neighbours in Muslim burkhas and, one by one, smuggled them into Panch Number.

The women went into hiding in his parents' third-floor flat. Nathni, the loyal Hindu darwan, who resembled a wrestler, abandoned his lathi and his post by the gate and squeezed his hefty frame under a four-poster mahogany bed. A young boy from the Hindu family hid inside a water tank on top of the roof, believing he would be safer. At sunset, after the muezzin's last cry of "Allah Ho Akbar," rose from the small mosque across the street, gangs of Muslim goondas began to prowl the streets. When they found the Hindu home deserted, they suspected what had taken place. They descended on Panch Number and demanded that the doorman Nathni and the other Hindus be sent out into the street. When the Hindus failed to emerge they poured petrol all around the house and threatened to burn it down. Obaidur, who had preceded his younger brother back to Calcutta, stood at the top of the spiral service stairs and hurled abuses at the hoodlums, calling them cowards and sons of pigs. Dulha Bhai joined him. If they dared to set fire to the house, he threatened, their families and their children would never again receive free medical treatment from him.

The mob, using the spiral stairs, forced their way up to the roof instead. They found the boy hiding in the water tank and dragged him into the street, where they stabbed him several times and left him to die.

Later that night, Dulha Bhai heard faint moans from the body still lying in the street in a pool of blood. Disregarding the curfew, he dashed out and carried the boy to his dispensary on the street corner and gave him whatever medical treatment he could till the youngster could safely be moved to a hospital. Miraculously the boy survived. Numerous stories of Hindus helping Muslims and Muslims helping Hindus slowly began to emerge from the wretched debris of the massacre. Years later, following Dulha Bhai's death, Pearl Road was renamed Dr. Ghani Road.

Once tears were wiped, and the newlyweds gently reproached for their ill-timed arrival, Abdul and Jameel, two skinny wide-eyed servants, were summoned to haul the trunks up to the third floor of the house my paternal grandfather had built for his growing family. Out of twelve children, however, only five had survived into adulthood.

My father's mother, a complete contrast to my dancing maternal grandmother, was the quintessential grandmother, a true "Dadi." She was petite; her finely chiselled face was framed with soft silvery waves. Her somewhat sad, sleepy eyes were magnified by gold-rimmed spectacles. She wore no make-up and, with the exception of two slim gold bangles, no jewellery. Her head was customarily covered with one end of a simple bordered white cotton sari. The house keys and money, tied into a knot of the palloo of her sari and then slung over her left shoulder, would jingle when she went about her daily chores. A heart-shaped silver paan-daan, containing leaves and other paraphernalia for preparing paan, was always within her reach. A faint fragrance of delicately scented betel nut followed her wherever she went, which was never very far.

Her rare excursions from the house were mostly to the Calcutta zoo, which was managed or owned by some distant relative. These Sunday outings, with her grandchildren in tow, involved her getting into purdah, walking down three flights of stairs, and sending Nathni to hail a palki-gari and bring it right to the front door.

She was rewarded for her efforts by a chimpanzee who puffed on a cigarette while swinging jauntily from tree limb to tree limb. When the children dragged her to visit the slithery pythons in the smelly reptile house, and to view the lazy crocodiles who would slyly slip into the water with a splash, she offered little resistance.

Normally there was little need for Dadi to step out of the confines of her spacious breezy bedroom. The world came to her.

The fruit-wallah came. The vegetable-wallah came. The egg-and bread-wallah came. The meat-wallah came.

When the box-wallah came to her door, hawking plastic hair clips, bracelets, ribbons and trinkets, and unfurling bolts of gaudy fabrics, Dadi would discreetly crumple rupee notes into the palms of her grandchildren's eager hands.

A Northerner, Jamila Khatoun was gentle, soft-spoken and fluent in both her native Urdu and her adopted Bengali. Yet she stubbornly upheld an ongoing feud with her husband by refusing to speak to him in his native Bengali, while Dada, who was also fluent in Urdu and equally stubborn, conducted his part of their daily bickering in

Bengali. One possible cause of discord might have been the endless hours my grandfather, a retired judge, whiled away playing games of solitaire. But when he died, at a respectably ripe age, Dadi withered away with grief.

Panch Number, a three-storied concrete structure built by my grandfather in 1936, had been designed by my father while he was a student of engineering at Kharagpur. The facade and cantilevered entry were inspired by the Metro Cinema in downtown Calcutta, which, upto that time, had been my father's only exposure to modern architecture.

My own recollections of Panch Number are blissful memories of a large house filled with cousins competing over games of ludo and snakes and ladders, games of hide 'n seek on the roof top, squabbling aunts, my uncle Kochi, who wrote poetry and accompanied himself on the harmonium while he sang Tagore's doleful songs, and was rumoured to be clinically insane.

Youngsters were discouraged from playing in the drawing room of one of the two second-floor flats. This was the sacred turf of Dulha Bhai's brother, Abu Sayeed Ayub, a tall, distinguished man with pale, translucent skin, and an air of serene abstraction. A writer and professor, Abu Sayeed had originally wanted to become a scientist; he was a disciple of Meghnath Saha and the Nobel Prize–winning physicist C.V. Raman. However, he eventually quit science and became a Gandhian. When he quit being a Gandhian, he became a Marxist. Disillusioned by Marxism, he ultimately poured his energies into founding and editing a literary journal, *Quest*. Ironically it was his brother, originally a student of the Koran and deeply religious, who ended up a true Marxist. Dulha Bhai joined the Communist Party of India and in the sixties did time in jail for his political beliefs and activities.

Abu Sayeed's musty, book-filled room was the hub of Calcutta's intellectual life. Each evening, wrapped in soft woollen shawls, and seated away from draughty windows, he received poets, writers, journalists, politicians. Abu Sayeed had the ability to argue for or against any topic with the likes of Buddha Dev Bose, Bishnu Dey, Humayun Kabir, Sudhin Dutta and Hiren Mukherjee. He converted my father into an atheist and an ardent devotee of Bertrand Russell. When he was quite certain my mother was no empty-headed dancing girl, he set out to educate and guide her as well. He threw open his library to her and guided her through the world of Gorky, Huxley, Maupassant, Tagore, Tolstoy and Lin Yutang.

Directly above Abu Sayeed's room was my grandmother's bedroom which, in later years, doubled as a museum for my mother's various trophies, awards, and family portraits including early pictures of my father, posing to look like Mr. Universe, in skimpy trunks, admiring his flexed biceps.

A pious Muslim, Dadi got down on her knees five times a day and faced Mecca to say her prayers. She kept roza, fasted during the month of Ramzan, and celebrated the festival of Id with culinary vengeance. Her main mission in life was coaxing succulent shami-kababs, muslin-thin roomali rotis, and sweet mango pickles down people's throats till they were at the point of exploding.

But unlike food, her religious beliefs remained her own and were never forced on anyone. She was resigned to the fact that her off-spring had arranged their own marriages. Her eldest son, Obaidur, had married an Estonian. Her middle son (my father) had married a "half-breed." One daughter had married her own cousin (Dr. Ghani), a grandson had married a Hindu, and her nephew, Abu Sayeed, had not only married a Hindu, but went so far as to hyphenate his wife's last name to his own.

The ultimate test of her tolerance arose from my own youthful ignorance. Once, on a short trip to Calcutta with my mother during one of her dance engagements, we had paid a visit to the city's famous Kali temple. My mother suggested we keep our expedition secret from my father's family, especially from my profoundly orthodox Muslim grandmother, who'd be horrified to learn we had visited the temple where humans were once sacrificed. But when we returned to Panch Number, I was still overwhelmed by my encounter with the enigmatic goddess. The Brahmin priest who led us to view Kali in the sanctum of the temple had recited some mantras, then smeared my forehead with a bloody vermilion paste that trickled down to the tip of my nose. He removed a garland of hibiscus and tuberoses from the neck of the awesome black goddess and placed it around my own neck. My hair stood on end, I was covered with goose bumps. I felt my own tongue was red and bloody and hanging hungrily out of my mouth. Kali's cruel smiling eyes bore right through me and took complete possession of me. I felt elated and terrified, all at the same time. I had an uncontrollable urge to share my fantastic experience with my grandmother, who had by then gone blind. My mother looked horrified, as I started to tell Dadi how we'd spent the afternoon, but the words kept tumbling out.

I had never given my grandmother a gift. In fact, I had indulged in petty thievery: stealing spoonfuls of condensed milk that was specially put aside for her tea, and during the month of Ramzan, quietly helping myself to her little dish of sprouted beans with fresh ginger and lemon, which was the first solid food she would eat when she broke her fast at sunset. Now, while my mother frantically gesticulated her disapproval, I removed the garland that was still around my neck and placed it in Dadi's hands. She became very quiet, and then took the garland of hibiscus and tuberoses and hung it on her bedpost.

"I will dry your flowers from Kali and keep it in my Koran forever," she said. That was my last memory of her.

My father believed an old family curse had forced his mother to accept her lot philosophically.

According to the story, Dadi's somewhat rakish younger brother had once invited her daughter for a ride in a Tiger Moth he was test-flying for a race to London.

"Don't you dare let your daughter fly in that contraption," Dadi's father warned. "Before you know it your children will be eating pork. Next thing they'll be crossing the ocean and marrying foreigners and non-believers and, Allah forbid! one might even end up with a dancing girl for a wife!"

Needless to say, Dadi's daughter, my father's eldest sister, went ahead with her little joyride.

While the family was not subjected to Dadi's religious beliefs, it was impossible to escape her superstitions. Jingling keys foreshadowed a fight; opening an umbrella inside the house brought on misfortunes;

if you made a face or crossed your eyes the wind would stick that expression for life; if you sat on a pillow you would get boils on your bottom.

My mother, trapped in a strange house by frequent curfews and the unpredictability of roaming mobs, often passed the time by stitching simple baby clothes for my impending arrival. One afternoon Dadi found these drying on the roof. She grabbed them off the clothesline and flung them away.

"Tobaa! Tobaa! Shame on you! Don't you know anything? It's bad luck to prepare anything for a baby before it's born," she shrieked completely baffling her daughter-in-law who could understand neither Urdu nor Bengali.

During a rare spell of calm in the city, some members of the family took my mother out to K.C. Das to try their famous Bengali sweets. To compensate for long stretches during the rioting, with no food to eat in the house, she proceeded to sample practically every item listed on the menu.

Later that night, the prearranged alarm, a little brass dance bell hanging from my prospective parents' third-floor window to the window of the floor below, awakened Dulha Bhai, the doctor in the house.

My mother had been adamant about delivering her baby in a hospital. The city was under curfew, and the only way to reach the hospital was by ambulance. The ambulance, summoned by telephone, could not locate the house. Its siren could be heard in the distance, circling the neighbourhood. Despite a shoot-to-kill order, Dulha Bhai, looking like a local goonda in his crumpled lungi, ran into the streets yelling and chasing after the ambulance.

I was born at the Calcutta Nursing Home on the fourteenth of November 1946. My mother's initial delight at becoming a mother was short-lived—the prospect of returning to Panch Number and a house full of relatives filled her with misgiving. A home of her own, that was what she wanted when my father asked what would make her happy. Her own place where she could enjoy some privacy, be the boss, and more importantly, get back to the dancing she had put aside all these months.

Luckily, a friend visiting the nursing home had a friend who had an aunt who owned a building in a safe locality, not far from Panch Number.

After getting together some odds and ends of furniture on hire, my parents moved into their new home on Lower Circular Road during Christmas. My mother, now sixteen, suddenly found she was a rather competent woman of the house and took delight in shopping for curtains, towels, sheets, and pots and pans. Whenever she could keep a maid, the chores would be done, but every so often they would be scared away by all the work and run off.

By the time Ayah joined the household, the joys of motherhood had worn off and my mother was quite ready to pour me out with the bath water.

The talk at the time was only of Partition.

There was to be no Pakistan for the Rahman family, though Ali, the husband of my father's youngest sister, and the husband of his niece, Dolly, opted for East Pakistan and moved with their wives to Dhaka.

In early March, Queen Victoria's grandson, Lord Louis Mountbatten, arrived in New Delhi to negotiate Britain's withdrawal from India. On the second of June the Indian National Congress officially agreed to the terrible price of freedom—a divided India.

On the night of 14 August 1947, standing on the rampart of that majestic remnant of the Moghul Empire, the Red Fort, in Delhi, Jawaharlal Nehru declared to a euphoric nation:

"Long ago we made a tryst with destiny, and now the time comes when we shall redeem our pledge, not wholly or in full measure, but very substantially. At the stroke of midnight, while the world sleeps, India will wake to life and freedom . . ."

Modern India awoke to a terrible carnage. Sikh and Hindu refugees fled the newly formed West Pakistan into India. Muslims fled India into West Pakistan. In Bengal, Muslims fled to East Pakistan, Hindus, from what had been East Bengal, fled to West Bengal. In Calcutta, a disillusioned Mahatma Gandhi threatened to "fast unto death" if riots broke out again in the city. He slept through the tumultuous events of 15 August in the burned-out home of a Muslim family.

The city responded to his pleas and remained calm.

But it took the bullet of a Hindu fanatic to finally stun the rest of India out of its bloody madness.

On the evening of 30 January 1948 Nehru announced on All India Radio:

> "The light has gone out of our lives and there is darkness every where, and I do not quite know how to tell you, or how to say it. Our beloved leader, Bapu, as we call him, father of our nation, is no more . . ."

A few weeks after the assassination, my father, recently appointed senior architect to the West Bengal government, was asked to design for the slain leader a modest, yet appropriate memorial on the banks of the Hooghly River where some of his ashes had been immersed. My father's design for Gandhi Ghat—a fusion of a simple Hindu temple spire, capped with an Islamic dome, and a cantilevered projection from either side of the spire forming a Christian cross— harmoniously symbolised India's major religions as well as Gandhiji's philosophy of love and tolerance.

At the dedication of the monument a year later, Jawaharlal Nehru, standing before thousands of spectators, started to shout for the architect. He grabbed my father's hands and exclaimed: "I congratulate you on your magnificent conception!"

9

Indrani

My mother launched into her dance studies as soon as we were settled in the new flat. There were no eminent gurus of Bharata Natyam in Calcutta at that time, but other forms of dance still flourished. Kathak had come on the scene as early as 1856 when Nawab Wajid Ali Shah of Oudh, an accomplished musician and Kathak dancer, was deposed by the British government for his neglect of affairs of state in favour of dance. They took over his kingdom and exiled him to Calcutta with a generous pension which he fueled into his continued patronage of Kathak. In 1920 Rabindranath Tagore discovered Manipuri, which was, until that time, unknown beyond the borders of Manipur, and brought a Manipuri dancer to teach his students at Shantiniketan. He adapted the soft, flowing elements of Manipuri to his own poems and songs and toured India with his disciples, adding stimulus to the revival of Indian classical dance.

Taking advantage of all Calcutta had to offer, my mother began to study both Kathak and Manipuri. She consulted Haren Ghosh, a noted Calcutta impresario, for advice on how to proceed with her future career. He advised her to specialise in one form of dance and concentrate on that. Some weeks later he invited her to a dance performance by Shanta Rao, a leading exponent of Bharata Natyam, whom he was presenting at Calcutta's New Empire Theatre.

The performance overwhelmed her; she came away with her mind set on studying Shanta Rao's elegant, classic Padanallur style of Bharata Natyam. My mother invited the dancer home for dinner and was so absorbed and fascinated by her that she couldn't remember a single question she had wanted to ask. Shanta, amused by the aspiring dancer's distraction, pointed out to her laughingly, that her breast milk, as she was trying to nurse me, was pouring down her arm onto the floor.

Some months later, my mother gathered courage and wrote to Shanta in Bangalore to ask if she could study with her, or perhaps with her guru, the renowned Padanallur Meenakshisundaram Pillai, in his village. Shanta wrote back a depressing letter discouraging her from pursuing a dance career. The dancer was quite blunt and said she couldn't imagine how a woman with a small child could survive the ordeals of village life and the gruelling physical demands and discipline of daily dance training.

The arrival of my American grandmother, finally, stepped up the search for the ideal guru. My father had stuck to his part of the bargain he had struck with Ragini Devi in New York and arranged for her to travel to Calcutta—a decision he would come to regret. The primary purpose of Ragini's return to India was to guide her daughter's dance studies and, with the help of a Rockefeller grant that she had been awarded, to conduct an all-India survey of religious festivals and rituals connected to dance for a more comprehensive book on Indian dance that she was planning to write.

Ragini took charge and went to work, renewing her old contacts in Bangalore. The famous dancer, Ram Gopal, who was also a disciple of Shanta's guru, suggested my mother first study the basics with U.S. Krishna Rao and Chandrabhaga Devi. This husband and wife team, who were also disciples of Meenakshisundaram and reputed to be fine teachers, were based in Bangalore where the climate and living conditions were comfortable.

Once all the arrangements were made, my mother was off to Bangalore. She moved in with the Krishna Raos and threw herself into her dance training right away. Her studies and expenses in Bangalore were financed jointly by my father and by a portion of Ragini's Rockefeller grant. Although he'd agreed to support her stay in Bangalore, my father began to fear he had lost my mother to dance. But since there was little he could do, he kept to his premarital promise not to interfere with her career. I was almost three and would often be dispatched, with Ayah, to Panch Number where I had plenty of cousins to play with and to fight with, while Ayah spent her time in the kitchen picking up culinary tips from Dadi and her cooks.

Daddy's fears heightened when my mother sent for me and Ayah to join her in Bangalore. After some months he could bear the separation no longer and followed us all to Bangalore. He had, at first, been in a state of great agitation, but once he saw her dance in a private debut performance in the reception hall of the Theosophical Society, at 6 St. Johns Road, he calmed down and gradually resigned himself to the fact that dance would come before all else: she was her art. This is how it would always be.

Whenever Mummy was home there was gaiety, laughter and excitement, but the times she was away dancing, gloom would set in, and my father would wait for her letters to arrive, and I would imagine each plane passing overhead was bringing my mother home.

And while Daddy was occupied at the office designing magnificent edifices, I depended on the servants for survival.

My mother's absences from home became more frequent as she was drawn deeper into her dance studies. Now she based herself in Madras where Ragini had arranged for her to study with Chokkalingam Pillai, son-in-law of Meenakshisundaram Pillai, and acclaimed to be one of the finest gurus of Bharata Natyam. Chokkalingam had at first been reluctant to take on a non–South Indian as a pupil, but his regard for Ragini, and for her role in reviving India's classical dances during the thirties, convinced him otherwise.

Although my mother felt privileged to be Chokkalingam's disciple, she sensed that he was holding back; she was hurt and wondered if his cool attitude towards her had something to do with her not being a Tamilian. One day she overheard him ask a fellow student, who was from a prominent Madras family, if her father's chauffeur could drive him to the market. He was returning to his village for the weekend, he said, and had wanted very much to buy a rocking horse for his grandson. The woman replied her father was busy that day and could not spare the car. My mother quietly returned to the St. Margaret Hostel at the YWCA where she and Ragini were staying, counted her few rupees, and took a rickshaw to the Moor Market and picked out a lovely, colourful rocking horse. She then stopped by her guru's hotel and had the rickshaw-wallah carry the rocking horse in and leave it there with the message that it was for Chokkalingam Pillai from Indrani. Just as she was about to leave, her guru, who must have been resting, came running out of the hotel dressed only in his dhoti and thanked her profusely with his hands folded. There was a change in the way he looked at her. His gratitude wasn't for the gift of the rocking horse but for her concern for him. From that day on he gave and gave, and held nothing back including sharp cracks on her shin when he was not satisfied with the results.

On 23 October 1950 Indrani had her arangetram at the Museum Theatre. Ragini wanted all of Madras to come to her daughter's official public debut. She ran to the editors of magazines and newspapers, and asked them to put Indrani's picture on the cover and write articles publicising her upcoming arangetram. They remembered Ragini well and opened their doors to her, offered her coffee and agreed to do whatever she wished.

Seated in the audience that night were all the leading dance connoisseurs, gurus and dancers of Madras—among them Balasaraswati, Tara Chaudhary, Vyjayanthimala, Yamini Krishnamurthy, Venkatachalam and Harin Chattopadhyaya.

Harin, who Ragini still refused to talk to, gushed over the performance: ". . . critics who understand the mechanics and subtleties of Bharata Natyam," he wrote, "prophesy an enviable future for the beautiful *danseuse* who is obviously gifted with grace and style worthy of that prophecy. A striking personality, vibrating with the colour and the perfume of authentic spring. Indrani is undoubtedly, in Keats' line, 'a thing of beauty is a joy forever'. . ."

In the Tamil publication, *Narada*, a critic wrote: "It was a surprise to all how a non-Tamil girl could have shown such abhinaya without long acquaintance with the language. We expect that Indrani will exhibit her art in many places in Tamil Nadu . . . Our Bharata Natyam will shine in North India through her, more and more."

10

Lower Circular Road

Our household was held together by two Muslim servants. Chand Banu Bibi, our ayah, was a tiny, yet feisty, young widow from Dhaka, who had come to my mother's rescue when I was three months old. She quickly made herself so indispensable that my family willingly endured the endless red-tape involved in employing her, as Ayah suddenly found herself, after Partition and Independence, an East Pakistani alien.

Our cook-cum-bearer, Johnny (Jaan Mohammed), picked up his name and fancy culinary skills while working for the US Army stationed in Calcutta during the war. His mutton "charps," lamb "strews," "fras beans," and "puteens" were panacea to my mother and father's fragile digestive systems, which were inhabited by some germs with a very long name.

Regardless of how the germs were behaving, a lightly spiced chicken curry, and a basmati rice pulau, cooked with saffron and plump raisins, appeared on the table at lunch every Sunday. Ayah, who helped Johnny in the kitchen, was convinced all the chickens sold in the market had died of some illness. So each Sunday morning, we were subjected to agonised squawks from the kitchen as she expertly beheaded a live chicken halaal-style.

Living on the ground floor of our building was a portly Armenian businessman and his equally portly family, headed by a grandmother who sat by the window and crocheted socks all day long. The flat above was occupied by a light-skinned, all-female family of dubious origins. An inquisitive neighbour kept track of the constant stream of businessmen entering and exiting the flat at odd hours. Aside from the Armenians, the ladies on the floor above them, and us, all the other tenants of the three-storied apartment building were Anglo-Indians. The oldest of the three children, living in the flat below us, told me one day when we were all skipping rope on our landing, that she and her family had lived in our flat before we arrived. They moved out because the flat was haunted. According to her, their aged grandmother used to sleep in what was now our drawing room. She had difficulty sleeping and each night she would pace up and down the room, out to the veranda and back. After she died in that room, they claimed, they could still hear her every night, shuffling back and forth.

I was convinced she was making all this up to frighten me, but one night, after a particularly raucous dinner party at our flat, one of my parents' close friends, a jobless poet-journalist, passed out in the drawing room. When Johnny brought his tea to him early the next morning, he was puzzled to find the man had vanished.

A few days later I overheard the journalist explaining his abrupt departure to my parents: he complained he had been awakened and chased away from the flat by the sound of someone shuffling to the veranda and back all night. Whether it was the whisky or the ghost we'll never know, but it was enough to scare the life out of me.

Our resident ghost began to haunt me in my dreams. I would see her perched on a high stool in one corner of the dining room, her wiry legs politely crossed. She was a horrible, toothless, sexless creature with pointed ears and an evil smile, and covered from head to toe with prickly, pinkish skin that resembled one of Ayah's plucked Sunday chickens.

What with the granny ghost in the dining room, and the bogeyman who, Ayah assured me, would haul me off if I didn't obey her every command, always lurking nearby, it took all the little courage I possessed to slip off to the veranda at night in hopes of catching the nightly entertainment.

Some time after dinner, a wiry Anglo-Indian gentleman, with slickly pomaded hair, and wearing the same well-worn, rayon suit each night, would appear on Lower Circular Road, armed with an accordion:

"Aana merri jaan, merri jaan," he would belt out the hit song from the 1947 film *Shehnai*.

"Sunday ke Sunday aana merri jaan . . . I love you!" People passing by on the street would stop and snap their fingers and whistle along to the nonsense "hinglish" love song.

"Mujhe Paris dikhao, mujhe London ghumao . . . Right, right, right. All right."

There were some who were less enthusiastic about his slightly off-key crooning and his nightly sign off invariably caused an uproar:

"Irene, good night, good night. Irene, good night. Good night Irene, good night Irene, I'll see you in my dreams . . ."

Mrs. Ghosh, a Bengali engineer's young German wife, who lived across the street from us, was not about to appear in anyone's dreams. Right on cue, she would throw open her window and yell:

"Oh! Vy don't you shut up, you bloody idiot! You have voken my baby up!"

"Irene" would flee, and we would have to listen to Mrs. Ghosh's baby scream all night. But the few coins the other neighbours threw down to him were well worth Mrs. Ghosh's abuses, and "Irene" would return each night for more.

Ayah objected to my hanging about the veranda at night. It was one of the many things that frequently aggravated her. Our daily battles were mostly a test of wills over how often I should bathe, what I should wear, and when, and how much, and what I should eat. Her prime goal was to fatten me up, since the fatter you were the more prosperous your family. The leading heroines, in the Hindi films Johnny took Ayah to see, all had healthy, chubby cheeks.

She'd divide the rice, dal and yogurt on my plate into little mountains and coax me to eat "one for Mummy, one for Daddy, one for Nani" and so on. When her bribery failed, she'd chase me around the house with a vile glass of warm Horlicks. But I got my revenge at night. Whenever my side of the bed we shared got cold and soggy I would force her to change places with me. Her idea of curing my bed-wetting was to sprinkle salt and rub my face in the foul-smelling sheets the next morning.

I had no official name at the time. At birth I was named Pritee, joy; but after several weeks of the household being kept up all night with my colicky crying, the joy must have gone out of that one. When my dancing grandmother arrived from New York she suggested Urvashi—a celestial dancer in Indra's heavenly court. Why that name didn't stick remains a mystery. The philosopher Abu Sayeed Ayub, my father's cousin and mentor, thought I should be called Nishaat, happiness. This name, distorted to a whiny, unhappy "Neesa" by Ayah, lasted the longest. Then one night, when I was about five, Mummy returned home from a dance performance she had attended at the New Empire Theatre, excitedly waving a programme that listed a dancer named "Sukanya." Suddenly I was the owner of yet another name.

It was impossible to remember or to live up to my new name, Sukanya (Sanskrit for good daughter), since the family never used it. I was "Baby" at birth and Baby even after I had produced my own babies. Ayah obstinately clung to Neesa, though whenever my bed-wetting was excessive she'd resort to calling me "Soo-Soo" Kanya.

But I would draw in my claws on those nights when we were securely tucked under the mosquito net and she'd launch into one of her storytelling moods. My favourite story was the one about the two brothers, Tuan and Tuin, who, due to a series of mishaps, are forced to hide in a large clay water pot which is soon carried off by a tiger hungry for small boys and sweet banana fritters. They wait for hours, in sheer terror, hoping for some passing hunter or woodcutter to come to their rescue. In the end it's not some gallant hunter or woodcutter who saves the day; it's the thunderous echo of the boys passing wind in the clay pot that sends the tiger fleeing.

I was curious about Ayah's own children. Did she miss them? Did they miss her? Of her several children only two had survived; one of her babies had died after swallowing a two-anna coin. The others most probably died of sickness and malnutrition, but she only talked about the one who had swallowed the coin. The modest salary she received from us each month was money-ordered to her remaining son and daughter who now lived in Dhaka with her widowed mother. The little extra cash she scraped together selling our used bottles and newspapers to the kabadi-wallah, was sometimes spent on buying me little gifts: dress materials on my birthday, and a fine pair of gold hoop earrings when I first had my ears pierced. Her own worldly possessions fit into a small, grey tin trunk, decorated with pink roses, which she kept stored under our bed.

In the early evenings, she used to walk me, and my duck (a short-lived pet that substituted for chicken one Sunday), to a nearby maidan where I could set the duck free to swim in the park's murky pond. While I occupied myself with games of "I sent a letter to my love" and "Oranges and lemons sold for a penny" with the other children, Ayah would gossip with other ayahs. They'd sit on their haunches and with much chortling and rolling of eyes proceed to compare their husbands' "things" to various vegetables—the sizes ranging from a puny, but potent, green chili to an impressive brinjal.

Ayah was slightly pockmarked and not terribly pretty, but this didn't discourage the somewhat dashing Johnny from romancing her . . . and getting nowhere.

She was the only person not to be impressed by the smart, white and gold turban he wore on nights my parents invited their friends over for dinner, an odd assortment of characters ranging from poets, painters, writers, smartly suited Bengali babus working for British firms, random relatives from Panch Number, to P.C. Sen, the pipe-smoking chief of police who'd arrive in his flying-squad jeep with the sirens blaring, escorted by an entourage of heavily armed guards. Johnny took great pride in passing around what he believed to be

American-style hors d'oeuvres: mostly cubes of tinned Kraft Cheese and cocktail onions skewered onto toothpicks embedded in a ball of dough, tinted red with some lethal dye. After serving dinner he would hover near the table, eagerly awaiting further orders.

Before I was old enough to join the grown-ups at the table, I had to contend with spying on them from behind my bedroom door, conveniently situated right off the dining room. On one occasion while I was feasting my eyes, a minor argument between my parents escalated into a full-scale war. Daddy shoved my mother's elbow off the table. She picked up a glass of water and threw it in his face. Johnny, a wicked grin on his face, dashed to the kitchen and returned with a bucket of water. He handed each a plastic bath mug and stood back to watch the sparks, and the water, fly.

A couple of nights later, when Ayah was helping Johnny chop onions in the kitchen, she suddenly ran out of the kitchen screaming "Bhoot, bhoot, bhoot." My father, hoping to avenge Johnny's aquatic chivalry, had pulled some costumes out of Nani's trunk, outfitted himself as a demon, and leapt into the kitchen from the servants' spiral staircase.

Ayah was not amused.

Another evening, the revelry came close to flying out of control. During a game of "Truth or Consequences," the poet-journalist, who had the run-in with our ghost, fearlessly opted for the consequences my mother was dishing out. His penalty was to march into the bathroom, through the bedroom I shared with Ayah, and pull the chain of the overhead flush three times. He kept crashing into the furniture as he staggered to the bathroom through our darkened bedroom. Ayah, who was almost asleep, started muttering abuses after hearing the drunken squeals and laughter that followed the first two flushes. The third flush was followed by a resounding crash and then silence. The metal water tank had fallen on top of the toilet and smashed it to a zillion pieces. The jobless journalist's life was spared by inches.

While he was relieved that the man was alive and unhurt, Daddy was also shaking with anger and rapidly calculating what it would cost to repair the damage. Just as the party was about to disintegrate on this glum note some wise soul poured him a whisky-soda and then got everyone laughing again with a side-splitting imitation of Nehru giving a flowery, sing-song speech in Hindi which began with something like: "Brothers and sisters! Our country should now move ahead, we should not go backwards . . . and we should definitely not go sideways . . ."

By this time my father had recovered his composure somewhat and had been cajoled by my mother into doing his "Martha Graham" for the guests. He retreated into the bedroom briefly and when he reappeared in the drawing room, he was draped in a bright, red silk sari, his torso bare, and his long, wavy, black hair parted down the middle. The dozen or so guests, excitedly anticipating what was to follow, moved back chairs and tables to make room for him.

Daddy placed himself in the centre of the stage that had been cleared and stood absolutely still with his eyes closed, as if deep in meditation. Then with a dramatic swish of red silk and eyes flashing he flung himself to the floor. He crawled and lunged and leaped, threw his arms up, drew them back to his chest, any anger left in him, washed well out of his system. He was, by this time, perspiring profusely and gasping for breath while I died with shame, peeking from behind the drawing room curtain. To my astonishment his audience was enthralled; they hooted with laughter, shouted "bravo," and applauded. It was not his intention to poke fun at Martha Graham whom he genuinely admired and had respected since his student days in America. He did, however, frequently remind friends that the only reason he had become an architect and not a dancer was that he wanted to spare his wife competition in the family.

His audience demanded an encore.

Daddy eagerly cranked up the gramophone and then, to the slightly scratchy strains of Katchaturian's "Sabre Dance," began to leap up and down vigorously, swinging his arms from side to side. This dance, which was once favourably reviewed in the New York papers, was his standard finale.

While my mother coaxed others into contributing their talents to the after-dinner entertainment, and acted as compere, she never danced herself, but if there happened to be a beautiful full moon, or if it was a rainy or stormy night, she and my father would break into one of Tagore's love songs. I couldn't fully understand the Bengali lyrics, but even the songs that sounded forlorn made me happy—happy because my parents were in harmony, the battle lines momentarily withdrawn.

My grandmother didn't volunteer her talents either. But her return to Calcutta, the scene of some of her earlier triumphs, rekindled in her a passion to put together a troupe and perform once again. Unfortunately, by the early fifties, the dance scene in India, that she herself had helped revitalise, was changing. Audiences were being exposed to solo artists from different parts of India who specialised in one style of dance, and were becoming more educated and sophisticated. The variety programmes of a decade ago were no longer in vogue. Intimate friends felt she was long past her prime as a performer, yet she was adamant to recapture some of her old glory. She threw together a small troupe, which included my mother, and some local dancers who had once danced with Uday Shankar, and with money borrowed from my father she booked herself into the New Empire Theatre.

The day of the performance was filled with last-minute rehearsals and preparations. There were frantic calls to make sure the press had been issued passes. Ayah was sent off to the market to buy garlands and fresh flowers for the dancers' hair. It seemed a miracle when dancers, musicians, instruments and costume trunk were finally crammed into a taxi headed for the theatre.

Ayah and Johnny were enjoying a rare moment of peace and quiet when the frantic ringing of the doorbell broke the silence. It was my grandmother and mother in a state of frenzy. Apparently, in the midst of the chaos, the trunk filled with all the costumes and ornaments had been forgotten in the boot of the taxi.

I thought it wisest to dissolve into the background while they ransacked the flat for all the saris and jewellery that looked glittery enough for the stage. Despite the fiasco and low spirits, they somehow managed to get through the evening.

Early next morning the Sikh taxi driver, grinning happily, turned up at the door with the costume trunk intact. Catching another glimpse of the two foreign-looking ladies was all the reward he hoped for.

11

Miss India

One late winter afternoon in 1952 an unexpected visit to our flat by a delegation of ladies, led to events my mother would spend the rest of her life trying to erase from memory.

Ayah had barely finished passing around glasses of her ubiquitous lemon squash when the spokeswoman of the group revealed the purpose of their visit. They were scouring Calcutta for beautiful girls from respectable, upper-class families to compete in the newly established Miss Calcutta beauty pageant. Two winners would be selected and flown to Bombay to participate in India's first ever "Miss India" contest. The lucky winner of the Miss India title, and her chaperone, would be flown on an all-expense-paid trip around the world to Hollywood. Then at Long Beach, California, she would join a line-up of international lovelies to compete in the world-famous Miss Universe pageant. The contestants would also be treated to a VIP stay in New York, be wined and dined by the mayor, and meet with the secretary-general of the United Nations, Trygve Lie.

"The contest," the lady explained, "is being sponsored by E.S. Patanwalla, manufacturers of 'Afghan Snow Beauty Aids', and by Pan American Airways and Catalina Swimsuits. In addition, Universal-International Studios will present Miss Universe with a seven-year movie contract with a starting salary of $250 per week in US dollars!"

My mother declined their offer. "Thank you for thinking of me. I'm quite flattered. But I'm an artist, you see, a classical dancer. I have no desire to take part in any beauty pageants or to become a movie star. In any case it will be quite impossible. I'm a married woman with a five-year-old daughter!"

"That's no problem, my dear," the spokeswoman of the group insisted, pulling out a sheaf of papers from her bag. "It states clearly here in the official guidelines that the regional, the national as well as the international contests are open to girls between the ages of eighteen and twenty-eight. It matters not whether they are single, married, widowed, divorced, or whether they do or don't have children. Judging will be on the basis of beauty of face and figure, poise, charm and personality."

"Thank you. But it's not for me."

The ladies were puzzled by my mother's complete lack of interest and sudden air of superiority. Announcement of the beauty contest had sent girls across Calcutta flying to their mirrors. Bolder and more optimistic ones filled out entry forms and demanded to have their measurements taken by the selection committee. The ladies were now worried that the wrong type of girls, with questionable moral credentials, were being attracted to the contest.

Just as they were about to give up, and exit in a flurry of chiffon and French perfume, my father returned from the office. They pounced on him. They pleaded that he try to convince his wife to participate. The contest, they assured him, would be devoid of vulgarity. The girls would not be required to parade around in bathing suits, they would compete wearing saris. Highly educated and cultured ladies like Lady Rama Rao, Mrs. Mary Clubwallah and Mrs. Kutty Ramanyya had expressed an interest in the contest which, they further assured us, was for a good cause. The entire proceeds of both the Calcutta and the Bombay contests were being donated to The Society for the Rehabilitation of Crippled Children, and to India's only polio clinic.

With an encouraging nudge from my father, who thought it all quite harmless, my mother succumbed, and from then on, the contest was a huge lark for her. The victorious ladies marched off to try to recruit the lovely, half-Scot-half-Bengali daughter of West Bengal's chief engineer.

On 26 March, the night of the Miss Calcutta competition, curious crowds thronged Calcutta's fashionable Chowringhee Road and clustered around the main entrance to the posh Grand Hotel, pushing and shoving and feverishly trying to steal a peek at Calcutta's beauties and its high society. The Princes' ballroom was packed to capacity. Colourful posters with enticing pictures of Hollywood and New York advertising the upcoming Miss Universe contest were pinned to a curtain behind the raised platform in the hall's centre.

The ballroom was festooned with balloons, streamers and confetti. Bearers, dressed in crisp white tunics with red and gold cummerbunds, shuffled noiselessly between the potted aspidistra palms and wicker chairs, balancing trays of spiced cashews and drinks. On this occasion, much to my delight, my mother carted me along without my having to throw the usual tantrums. I disliked being left behind with Ayah and Johnny when my parents went out in the evenings, and would work myself into a frenzy, envying all the fun they were having without me. Normally, when my parents prepared to spend an evening out they would either discuss their plans in Bengali, which was hard for me to follow, or they would announce that they had to meet some boring "contact." One evening they slipped off for a boring contact more grandly dressed than usual. I became suspicious and kicked and screamed and rolled on the floor till Johnny put me in a taxi and carried me, in my pajamas, to an elegant restaurant, with a live band, where my parents were partying with a rather jolly group of architects visiting from abroad. Johnny deposited me there and fled before my parents could call him back—while I, content at last, fell sound asleep on a banquette next to my horribly embarrassed parents.

The evening of the beauty contest, Ayah had dressed me up in a lovely South Indian silk ghaagra and blouse that had been tailored for me in Bangalore. While I was completely engrossed, gawking at the dazzling line-up of forty beautiful young ladies parading around in gorgeous silk brocade and wispy chiffon saris, Maya Guha, the daughter of the chief engineer, was selected first runner-up, and my mother was crowned Miss Calcutta.

In an instant she was mobbed by photographers with cameras flashing, and by reporters all talking at once and scribbling notes. I was a little frightened by the whole business and, standing there by myself, wished my father had come along as well. But it was chiefly a ladies' charity affair that my mother, still, did not take seriously, and had not pressed him into coming.

Mummy finally emerged through the crowd, laughing and clutching on to a crown that looked like something Ole King Cole might have worn. To celebrate her victory, she announced she was taking me to Firpos, Calcutta's classiest restaurant, and I could order anything I wanted. We were given a table by the window, Chowringhee was spread below us. I had a gigantic hot fudge sundae and generous sips of my mother's sherry, oblivious of all the curious stares.

Ayah and Johnny had retired for the night by the time we returned home. Daddy had fallen asleep in a chair and was snoring loudly as the radio blasted Rabindra Sangeet. Mummy still had her crown on, and the Miss Calcutta sash was pinned to her sari. She turned off the radio, nudged him awake, and demanded to be congratulated. Daddy jumped up with a start. He brought out a bottle of Rémy Martin that he had been saving for a special occasion, and while they celebrated, I went off to bed in all my finery. The next morning, Daddy, dressed in the crown and Miss Calcutta sash, brought Mummy her morning coffee in bed.

Much to Ayah's annoyance I was allowed to stay home from school without having to hide under the bed or fabricate the usual bellyaches or headaches. Johnny loved the added excitement in the household, though Ayah thought this beauty contest business was a lot of nonsense, it would invite the evil eye: "Mummy ko nazar lagega."

The next day my father broke out in hives and collapsed, barely able to breathe. Mummy became hysterical. She phoned Dulha Bhai at his clinic and asked him to come right away. Babu had come down with an "attack of bumps," she explained. Within minutes, almost all the inhabitants of Panch Number, including my elderly grandparents, landed up in our flat, wailing and crying. They thought my father had been killed in a "bomb attack." Dr. Ghani diagnosed the bumps as a severe attack of urticaria, an allergic reaction to something he might have eaten earlier, and prescribed some antihistamines. But Dadi claimed it was an omen. The good fortune of the beauty contest needed to be balanced by the bad.

With one flash of a camera, our lives had changed. Before we had a chance to absorb any of it, Mummy was whisked off by plane to Bombay. Calcutta's daily papers were filled with stories and pictures of the contest. Announcement of the Miss India beauty contest had led to protests and demonstrations throughout the country. Conservative politicians proclaimed Indian women should not be made to parade their assets. They imagined innocent Indian women being trapped by sinister foreigners into secret sessions of debauchery. Communists and Leftists denounced evil Yankee capitalists for, as one senior politician complained, "trading on the flower of Indian womanhood."

In spite of all the negative publicity—or, more likely, because of it—ten thousand people turned up at Brabourne Stadium in Bombay. As promised, there were no bathing suits. All contestants were modestly attired in saris. Contrary to the sponsors' fears and expectations, even spectators in the cheaper stalls behaved well and joked amiably with the girls.

According to newspaper and magazine articles, the ceremony at the stadium opened with an impressive parade of massed bands of the Army, the Navy and Bombay Police marching in formation. The parade was followed by displays of physical culture by boys from the Bombay Barbell Club and girls trained by Dr. Sarkari's Health Home.

As judges voted by secret ballot, contestants were paraded around the stadium in gaily-decorated Cadillac convertibles, interspersed with floats of various commercial sponsors. The Pan American Airways float depicted a floral insignia of their trade emblem: wings, floating through clouds, surrounded by nymphs clad in the airline colours. Universal Pictures' float recreated scenes from their movie *The Prince Who Was a Thief*, that starred Tony Curtis and Piper Laurie. The Associated Watch Co.'s float was headed by a gigantic swan dominating a court scene with dancers performing to their own portable music.

My 21-year-old mother was taken completely by surprise when S.K. Patil, then mayor of Bombay, amid loud cheers and shouts, announced her name and called her up to the dais to be crowned India's first "Miss India." Bollywood queen Nargis, and her leading man, matinee heart-throb Raj Kapoor, joined the newly-elected beauty queen and the mayor in a specially reserved Cadillac which paraded them around the stadium and the city.

Miss India returned to Calcutta with a gem-studded gold crown, a gold trophy, a gold watch, an Olivetti typewriter, a Murphy radio, an endless supply of very sweetly scented Afghan Snow face cream, and assorted lipsticks and rouges (which I eventually inherited), and the grand prize—two tickets around the world on Pan American Airways.

Newspapers were clamouring for interviews. Film offers were pouring in from Bombay, and as the telegrams and letters arrived, Mummy consigned them to the dustbin. Stars like Dilip Kumar, Dev Anand and Raj Kapoor were bewildered anyone would want to turn down an opportunity for the staggering fame and fortune a Bombay film career guaranteed. My mother, while she was thrilled at winning the contest and all the fabulous prizes, was eager to distance herself from the Hindi film world. She feared the whole beauty queen business would tarnish her rising reputation as a serious classical dancer. Ragini, on the other hand, was convinced that the publicity would only add to my mother's fame as a dancer.

Our daily life required adjustments. My mother and I could no longer jump into a cycle rickshaw and go off on our shopping sprees to New Market without hordes of people chasing after her for her autograph and shouting "Miss India! Hey! Miss India!"

I resented sharing her with these pushy strangers. I felt protective and stuck my tongue out at the street Romeos who'd wink and whistle and follow her around. Once, when we were returning from a shopping expedition, my mother supplemented my efforts by reaching out of the rickshaw and thrashing an overly persistent fan with her parasol. We had to stick to travelling in rickshaws since taxis remained an indulgence—my parents achieved fame in their lifetime but fortune remained elusive. Mummy took to wearing sunglasses, and covered her head with the end of her sari. This might, at any rate, have been necessary since her hair had turned a bright green!

A distant relation of my father's, who had for some reason taken an immediate dislike to my mother, delighted in getting her all worked up. "You know you are quite good-looking," he had told her after dining at our flat one evening. "But your lightish brown hair makes you look like a foreign memsahib. How can you flaunt yourself as Miss India?"

My mother, fortified by several pegs of rum, bristled with rage. Her eyes flashed lightning bolts. "You sonofabitch. Out! Out! Get out of my house. THIS MINUTE!"

Johnny, who had been standing close by, dashed to the kitchen and carried back buckets of water to the veranda to help my mother douse the banished guest as he fled down Lower Circular Road.

Nonetheless, she ran the next day to the Army-Navy War Surplus Store on Park Street and purchased a bottle of imported black hair dye. The bottle of dye had undoubtedly been sitting on the shelf for a good part of the century; it turned my mother's hair green. Not only that, it turned stiff as cardboard. It wouldn't wash out. Ayah tried softening it with coconut oil. It wouldn't soften. For the first time in her life, my mother splurged on a beauty parlour.

"Madam, if you had come to us to begin with," the young Chinese hairdresser said rather smugly, "this would never have happened. You will simply have to wait for the hair to grow out."

Despite the green hair, my mother's pictures were plastered across the country on billboards, magazines, even candy boxes. Fortunately, in the black and white pictures it didn't show up green; in the colour pictures her hair was cleverly tinted black.

The advertisements filled me with a mixture of pride and embarrassment, but my father delighted in teasing Mummy whenever her picture popped up somewhere. There were pictures of my mother holding a teacup and extolling the virtues of Lipton Tea. There were pictures of her admiring a pair of Bata sandals on her feet. The one that made me want to go into hiding was a larger-than-life picture of her, reclining coyly on a mattress, declaring to the nation, "Dunlopillo is the most comfortable cushioning in the world!"

12

Nani

Ayah and I were packed off by train to Bangalore, a few days before my parents departed on their Pan American Airways trip around the world. My grandmother, who was then sixty, had finally torn herself away from the stage and was now settled there, researching and writing her book on Indian dance.

Unlike sweltering, crowded, cacophonous Calcutta, Bangalore was clean and tranquil, the climate mild, the air fragrant with languid breezes carrying whiffs of jasmine and frangipani. The prospect of living there for a whole month, with my grandmother all to myself, filled me with great excitement.

Nani's modest bungalow on Brigade Road was surrounded by an enticing garden shaded by guava, papaya and jackfruit trees, all heavy with fruit. I looked forward to spending blissful days exploring this paradise, climbing the trees, feasting on fresh fruit—far from Ayah's tentacles.

My grandmother, it turned out, had entirely different plans for me. Before I could slip off to compete with the crafty tribe of monkeys monopolising the trees, Nani hauled me into her cramped drawing room and led me to a dark bronze image of the goddess Kali squeezed in between some dusty books on a shelf. Curtains drawn across the two small windows in the room blocked the brilliant morning sun. Nani put a match to a wick in a brass lamp filled with coconut oil, lit a few sticks of Mysore sandalwood incense, and scattered a handful of freshly picked red hibiscus buds by Kali's feet. The flame flickered, and swirls of sweetly scented smoke rose into the air.

She then instructed me to join my palms together, close my eyes, and pray for my mother to win the Miss Universe contest.

I followed her orders. But when I finished praying and opened my eyes a shiver ran up my spine: the goddess seemed to be smiling at me. As my eyes gradually grew accustomed to the dark I could make out a garland of skulls hanging from her neck. Around her waist was a girdle of human hands. In one hand she carried a sword, in another a severed human head. Sharp fangs and a lolling tongue protruded from her mouth; she appeared to be thirsty for blood, yet her eyes were filled with kindness. She was ferocious and seductive, cruel and serene. I was confused, paralysed by fear, and unable to utter a sound.

What Nani saw in this enigmatic creature—who embodied fertility and destruction, who haunted the cremation grounds at night and had goats slaughtered in her honour at her temples—was a mystery to me. The only power Kali had over me was the power of terrifying me to death. Once a year on the last day of the Kali Puja festival, flat-bed lorries would thunder down Lower Circular Road carrying larger-than-life clay images of the many-armed goddess accompanied by frenzied devotees who beat drums and cymbals and sang and danced as they led her to the banks of the muddy Hooghly River for ritual immersion.

I could have hidden in my room and ignored the whole business. But blood-curdling yells of "Jai Bhadra Kali," "Victory to Kali," and the hypnotic beating of distant drums announcing yet another procession, kept luring me back to the veranda the way my prized horseshoe magnet lured the pins and needles and nails scattered on a floor.

Perhaps Kali could sense that I was terrified of her, perhaps she simply didn't hear my prayer, perhaps my mind was wandering, but a buxom blond from Finland, and not my mother, was crowned Miss Universe.

Nani, who had missed out on all the Miss Calcutta and Miss India commotion, was further devastated. "Your mother never listens to me," she complained. "If she had taken me along as chaperone instead of your father, she'd be wearing that goddamn crown today. You have to pull strings in America, campaign like hell, make sure you get all the publicity you can. I still have influential contacts in America, you know."

Despite her disappointment Nani forgave Kali. She offered her more hibiscus buds and more incense, hoping to ensure her future prayers would fare better. Before long the whole Miss Universe business was set aside, and Nani launched into her next campaign, while my parents continued their trip around the world, travelling on to Japan.

At breakfast the next morning, while I was going through the ordeal of swallowing the obligatory glass of hot milk which had a way of coming to life in my stomach, I could feel her eyes boring through me. A lipstick-stained cigarette dangled from one corner of her mouth, there was a determined glint in her eyes. Lightbulbs seemed to be turning on inside her head. She gulped down her coffee, stubbed out her cigarette, jumped up, and dragged me out to the veranda.

We pushed some chairs aside and cleared a space. Nani removed her slippers, hitched up her sari and tucked it into her petticoat. I stood before her and following her instructions joined my palms together as if in prayer. "Bend from the waist and touch the floor, keep your knees straight, like this," she demonstrated. "Place both hands on your hips, palms facing out. Now bend your knees, lift your right foot and stamp."

"Tei ya tei. Tei ya tei. Tei ya tei.
Tei ya tei—tei tei ta. Tei ya tei—tei tei ta."

She hammered out a beat with a wooden baton, recited the rhythmic syllables, and commenced to drill into me the basics of Bharata Natyam.

Each step had to be repeated in single, double and triple time. My heels ached, my calves ached, my thighs ached, the milk sloshed about in my stomach and began to curdle. While the monkeys ransacked the ripe guavas, papayas and jackfruit I struggled to learn the complicated alphabet of hand gestures and memorise their names in Sanskrit. Nani's current mission was to ensure the continuity of the family dance legacy.

It had all seemed so effortless when my mother danced. So far the extent of my dance experience, other than watching her, was limited to a school function in Calcutta. It was the high point of my brief spell at a girls' school, run by Mrs. Clark—a cheery, buxom Englishwoman, with large, protruding teeth, who dressed in gaily printed frocks. I was one of six little milkmaids who sang and danced to "Where are you going to, my pretty maid?"

It didn't arouse any grand passion in me to follow in my ancestral footsteps, but getting up on stage in costume and make-up appealed to me enormously.

These morning sessions on the veranda turned into a daily ritual. I was ashamed to admit to Nani that I was in agony. I plodded on bravely despite my sore muscles. Every now and then I'd peek at the trees longingly. Being alone, high up in a tree, was almost as satisfying as being able to spread one's wings and fly.

Ayah, who believed dancing was a waste of valuable time, took pity on me. One afternoon, instead of my mandatory nap, she took me along to see a Hindi film. We both sobbed at the injustices the beautiful but poor heroine endured at the hands of her rich, handsome lover's villainous father. We returned home humming the catchy tunes of the heartbreaking, song-and dance-filled film. Nani, who had tried to discourage this afternoon expedition, quickly put a stop to our frivolity.

"You are filling your head with garbage!"

She pointed out that the steps and gestures she was taking such pains to teach me were in strict accordance with the *Natya Shastra*, the ancient Sanskrit treatise on the science of the arts. She was well-versed in the chapters pertaining to classical dance. She ran to her bookshelf and pulled out a book. Right next to Kali were two copies of *Nritanjali*. "I wrote this book in 1928," she announced proudly. "It's the first book on Indian dance ever published in English.

"What I'm passing on to you is art. These dances are sacred. The dancing in Hindi films is mindless entertainment and cheap and trashy and vulgar!"

She pulled out photographs of fantastically costumed dancers she had recently seen perform in remote villages of Kerala during festivals honouring Goddess Bhagavati, the Divine Mother. The various representations of Kali were more awesome and terrifying than the image on her mantle. Black eyes popped out of wildly painted faces, fangs twirled out of sinister mouths. Some dancers wore ferocious carved wooden masks which were painted and decorated with seashells, and framed by gigantic headdresses fringed with peacock feathers. My grandmother trembled with excitement as she sifted through her bizarre collection of photos.

There were no limits to Nani's preoccupation with classical Indian dance. When Nani took me to the Raymon Circus I thought we would enjoy a brief respite from dance. I was holding my breath, waiting for the much touted lady to come flying out of the mouth of a canon. Just as the body, sheathed in a sequined, pale blue body suit, went hurtling through the air, Nani grabbed my right hand and began pulling my fingers.

"You need to work on your Tripataka Hasta."

She chose this earth-shaking moment to remind me that I had been bending all five fingers in the second (and trickiest) of the single-hand gestures. "When the hand is in Tripataka, only the ring finger should be bent in half, the rest must remain absolutely straight and held close together."

Another time we were strolling along Brigade Road before dinner one evening, when Nani suddenly stopped in front of a grocery store that was operated by a rather intimidating Englishman. She got completely carried away demonstrating the precise coordination of the Tripataka hands with the neck, the head and the feet. She flung out her arms, stretched one leg to the side, banged her heel on the pavement, and recited breathlessly:

"Tei yum tatta tei ta—tei yum tatta tei ta.
Tei tei dit dit tei—tei tei dit dit tei."

I edged away from her and pretended I belonged with a respectable South Indian family commenting on the display of under-ripe, over-priced apples wrapped in fine tissue paper.

It didn't matter to my grandmother if people stared at us as if we were mad. It didn't matter to her if her costly silk sari slipped in the back and dragged along the sidewalk.

I would have pointed such things out to my mother without hesitation, but with my grandmother there was a certain formality to our relationship. She was the only member of my family who called me "Sukanya," a name she could picture on posters and billboards.

After my dance class one morning she took me aback with an unusual display of affection, her special butterfly kiss (eyelashes fluttering on my cheek), and then handed me a bulky package, which I presumed was some dance-related gift. Instead, I found it contained a real toy—a large, brightly striped top that hummed and kept perfect balance as it spun round and around and around.

My grandmother seemed to be in cheerful spirits. That evening she hummed some song while she bathed and got all dressed up. She changed into an orange and gold sari, put on her flashiest earrings, and tucked a frangipani blossom behind one ear. I was gazing at her reflection in the mirror admiring the overall effect when a man's voice sent me flying to the veranda.

"Yoo hoo! Anybody home?"

Walking jauntily up the garden path was a smartly suited, muscular, dark-skinned gentleman from Goa, who looked a good many years younger than my grandmother. Tucked under his arm was a parcel wrapped in newspaper that turned out to be a bottle of XXX rum. I was sent off to bed earlier than usual while Nani and her visitor retired to the veranda, where they sat laughing and gossiping, smoking Charminars and drinking endless glasses of rum and Coca-Cola late into the night. For all I know, it might have been a perfectly innocent friendship. At the time I knew nothing of the string of lovers my grandmother had left in her wake. Harin, the great love of her life, visited us often in Calcutta, but never when Ragini was present. However, Ragini did keep up a friendship with both Jagtiani and Gopinath, who had gone on with their lives and apparently didn't harbour any feelings of remorse.

The Goan turned out to be a regular fixture. Ayah was certain the man was a scoundrel, and claimed she had seen him make passes at the sassy young servant girl who helped Nani with the house cleaning. Nani refused to believe Ayah and accused her of being jealous of the younger, prettier girl. It was many years later that I found out that some time after Ayah and I had returned to Calcutta, the servant girl's belly had begun to swell suspiciously. Nani sent the Goan packing. The girl, it seems, threw herself at Nani's feet and wept and begged for mercy. Nani, in a rare fit of restraint, resisted the urge to strangle her. Instead she sent her off to work for an "open-minded" Parsi lady in Bombay.

Camping in cramped quarters with two strong-willed, highly opinionated women was a continuous challenge. Bickering between Nani and Ayah was incessant. When Ayah complained about inadequate cooking facilities and the bland meals the room-boy brought to us on trays from a neighbouring Anglo-Indian social club, Nani screamed at her and told her she was welcome to return to Calcutta. Another battle erupted the day Nani accused Ayah of stealing her one-hundred-rupee false tooth. The house was turned upside down. We were all on our hands and knees hunting for the tooth that Nani had, herself, stashed away in a drawer for safekeeping. In retaliation, Ayah, a devout Muslim, carried on about the evils of idol worship. What was a white-skinned, Christian woman doing praying to half-naked, heathen images? Outsiders, filled with similar curiosity, were more diplomatic.

"I was a Hindu in a previous life," Nani would state grandly to people who wondered how she had become so involved with India and Indian dance. "I have been reincarnated to dance!"

13

The Dance of Shiva

Our five years at Lower Circular Road came to an unexpected close in the spring of 1953 when my father was offered the position of senior architect to the Government of India in New Delhi.

Leaving the familiar surroundings of our Calcutta flat filled me with anxiety, but my mother could not have been happier with the move to India's capital. The carnage and rioting that had welcomed her to Calcutta in 1946 remained indelibly etched in her memory. More importantly, she was eager to establish her name as a serious classical dancer, and determined to shake off the "stigma" of being the country's first "Miss India." Any mention of that title or the beauty contest was now strictly off limits.

Bharata Natyam, the style of dance she had chosen to perform, was still a novelty to North Indian audiences. Post-Independence India was exploding with nationalistic fervour, the cultural future still waiting to take shape; dance, music, the fine arts were in the process of rediscovery. New Delhi's newspapers were filled with announcements and reviews of dance performances, concerts of classical Indian music, and art exhibits by up and coming modern Indian painters. Such events were now vital ingredients in the city's fast-changing social and cultural landscape. Government leaders and bureaucrats were only too happy to comply with requests to inaugurate exhibitions, cut ribbons, and deliver long-winded speeches before performances.

Mummy wasted little time in settling us into our two sparsely furnished rooms in Constitution House, our temporary headquarters until my father was assigned a suitable government flat.

Partially concealed from the road by flowering hedges, filled with noisily chattering sparrows, the spartan barracks on Curzon Road had originally been thrown together to house British Army officers during the war. Monotonous rows of whitewashed rooms, fronted by a spacious veranda, branched off a long corridor divided by a central lounge and mess hall. Constitution House now provided housing for transient government officers, Members of Parliament, journalists, and a few odd artists.

With my parents invariably busy, I had only Ayah for company. She had travelled by train to Delhi with us, along with all our belongings that she and Johnny had also helped pack. Ayah was a solo act now as Johnny had chosen to remain behind in Calcutta where he had, thanks to our friend P.C. Sen, the chief of police, secured a steady job driving a van for the Calcutta police. To combat boredom I daily roamed the corridors of Constitution House on my tricycle. I was befriended by a Pakistani journalist, Zamir, and Saadi, the pretty Kashmiri social worker he was secretly romancing. They bought my silence with sandwiches and pastries ordered from the mess. I had a waving acquaintance with a large-sized man who sat at a typewriter all day, and could devour entire roast chickens by himself. My father later informed me he was Prithviraj Kapoor, veteran actor and Member of Parliament. Further down the hall, Elizabeth Bruner, a Hungarian painter, often invited me in for an Orange Crush. She resembled a gypsy fortune-teller in her brightly coloured Rajasthani skirts, handwoven shawls, long strands of glass beads, and her hair knotted haphazardly on top of her head. Her dark musty room was crammed with paintings of the Buddha, the Dalai Lama, and roses and irises and snow-capped mountains. A garland of faded marigolds was draped over a portrait of her mother, who had lived and painted in India. Bruner shared her cramped quarters with a vicious mongrel and a frail baby deer she was nursing back to health.

The dingy rooms, furnished with institutional Central Public Works Department sofas, chairs and beds, were brightened up with handloom spreads purchased at the Cottage Industries Emporium. My mother placed a small bronze image of a dancing Shiva Nataraja on the centre of the mantel. She laid her ankle bells before him, lit some sandalwood incense, and then glued herself to her Olivetti and started firing off letters to various "important contacts."

Before I'd wake up in the morning she'd have her lists all written up with names of people to call that day, letters to write, things to purchase. When she wasn't busy at the typewriter she was busy talking on the telephone. Her early morning phone calls to people generally began with "Oh! I hope I didn't wake you?" followed by an apologetic giggle when she got sleepy replies. Organisers of performances, directors of cultural societies, officials from the Ministry of Education and Culture, were soon trickling in and out of the microscopic drawing room, which, by night, reverted to the bedroom Ayah and I shared.

One of our first visitors at Constitution House was Kamala Devi Chattopadhyaya, who lived in a bungalow nearby, and helped organise my mother's first Delhi performance. I was ignorant, at the time, of her importance and her many accomplishments, which included establishing the Cottage Industries Emporium to promote Indian handicrafts. "I'm a boring old lady," she would say to me whenever she stopped by, "but I've known your Mummy since she was a baby, so you must come and sit and talk with me for a few minutes."

I hardly found her boring. Draped in bright silk saris, richly woven shawls, heavy jewellery, and glass bangles up to her elbows, she was a walking advertisement for the Indian handicrafts she treasured. She would take her time to form a sentence, and though she never missed a single party she was invited to, she would invariably nod off and start to snore right after eating.

Another frequent visitor was Venkatachalam, Ragini's old friend and saviour from Bangalore, who served on several powerful cultural committees around the country. Venka, who was also Kamala Devi's good friend, had a habit of turning up unannounced, with an assortment of his "waifs and strays of the better sort of both the East and the West." At times, included in his entourage was Harin Chattopadhyaya, Ragini's former lover and Kamala Devi's former husband, who usually made his entrance with some pretty young dancer attached to his arm. He'd keep us entertained all evening long with his latest poems and songs sung in a rich baritone. He remained an ardent fan of my mother's even though he couldn't claim her as his daughter. "Poetry in motion" was what he called her. Daddy offered his own take on the epithet, especially when someone was particularly clumsy, or suffering a bout of Delhi Belly.

One evening Venka showed up with a European gentleman who was married to a Punjabi interior designer, and touted to be a very important contact.

A cloud of smoke from his cigar enveloped him as he went around bowing gallantly before all the ladies, lifting their hands and planting sloppy wet kisses. A Jewish refugee from Budapest, Dr. Charles Louis Fabri was an eminent Indologist, a self-proclaimed Buddhist, and New Delhi's most influential art and dance critic. He had bulging, bespectacled eyes, and strands of curly blond hair strategically draped over several mysterious lumps on top of his head. He had originally travelled to India in 1931 to join Aurel Stein on archaeological expeditions along the Silk Route.

Ayah dashed about the room struggling to keep up with orders for lemon squash and endless pots of tea which she prepared in a makeshift kitchen at a corner of the veranda. Dr. Fabri helped himself to a glass of the lemon squash Ayah was passing around but declined the tasty onion pakoras she had just cooked up in the kitchen. Fried and spicy foods, Dr. Fabri explained in a thick Indianised Hungarian accent, caused him to pass wind. (He used the word Vayu, Sanskrit for wind.) He then proceeded to complain that our furniture, while artistic to look at, was hard and made his bottom sore. Despite the hazards of passing Vayu and suffering a sore behind, he became a regular visitor, and a vital force in propelling my mother to the forefront of Indian dance.

Charles was obsessed by beauty. He believed true art meant passion, "a deeply felt emotion, a total, restless devotion, at any price, to beauty . . ."

In *The Statesman* he described her performance for a delegation of visiting scientists as "possessing that crystalline quality of undiluted beauty and purity that makes a show forever memorable . . . In her [Indrani Rahman's] presentation of Bharata Natyam, this classical system has an exponent not only of great knowledge and utmost devotion but also of that other quality that is so difficult to achieve: beauty."

Clippings of these and other reviews were routinely dispatched to Ragini in Bangalore. Though she counted on her for artistic guidance, my mother generally discouraged Ragini from sitting in the audience when she performed. Dancing in front of her mother, she said, always made her nervous—a trait I later inherited.

Nani took great pride in her daughter's accomplishments but she also remained her severest critic and never allowed her to let the adulation go to her head. There was always room for improvement, she insisted. It was critical to keep up one's training under the leading gurus throughout a dancer's career, and to seek out and promote little-known dance forms.

By early May Delhi had turned into a furnace. The loo was blowing in from the Rajasthan deserts and covering everything with a fine coating of sand. Those who could afford it escaped to the hill stations. Ayah went off to Dhaka for a month to check up on her mother and two children. The kitchen on the veranda was shut down. We subsisted mainly on mangoes, succulent langra mangoes from Banaras for every meal. When Daddy wasn't slicing mangoes into cornflakes for us, he was busy at his drawing board, creating modern edifices for New Delhi. Mummy decided there was no better time to head for Madras, follow Ragini's advice and immerse herself in dance studies with her guru, and add new items to her repertoire.

She financed this study trip by selling a pair of gold bangles (a gift from her mother-in-law) to a Member of Parliament living a few doors from us.

Normally I would have stayed behind, but schools were closed and there was no Ayah to leave me with. My grandmother was busy working on her book and travelling through the jungles and villages of Bihar and Orissa researching different forms of Chhau dance, and anyway couldn't cope with me without Ayah's help. So it was settled I would travel to Madras, as well.

In Madras there was no one to leave me with either, so I sat, day after day, on the mud floor of the Indian Institute of Fine Arts at 72 Egmore High Road, and watched in agony as Mummy's guru, the venerable Chokkalingam Pillai, made her repeat over and over the rhythmic permutations to one line of song from a tillana he was teaching her.

The paper-thin walls and corrugated tin roof once again reverberated with beats of the guru's little wooden stick. The ferocity with which Chokkalingam attacked the small slab of wood sent little splinters flying in all directions. Rivulets of perspiration drenched my mother, nine soggy yards of her cotton sari clung to her limbs like cellophane wrap, a faint smudge was all that remained of the black tilak marking the centre of her forehead. The creaky ceiling fan was switched off. The cloying humidity and evil stench of an open sewer, which often permeated the city before an afternoon sea breeze picked up, was apparently preferable to muscle cramps and chills.

"Nadra dim tana, di ranaa—nadra daani tom ta di ranaa—nadra dim tana . . . ," her guru sang in a shaky, toothless voice. Wearing a white cotton dhoti, he sat cross-legged on a mat at one end of the room, his back erect, his chin jutting out with determination. If Mummy made a mistake, or if she didn't bend her knees enough, the seemingly benign old master would raise his small stick and smack her sharply on her shin.

The tillana, when danced without interruptions and at a tempo just fast enough to show off the elegant geometrical lines that characterised the Pandanallur style, was thrilling to watch, as was my favourite piece, a dance in praise of Shiva. Whenever Mummy practised

Indrani at the Miss Universe contest, Long Beach, California, 1952
Photos: Habib Rahman

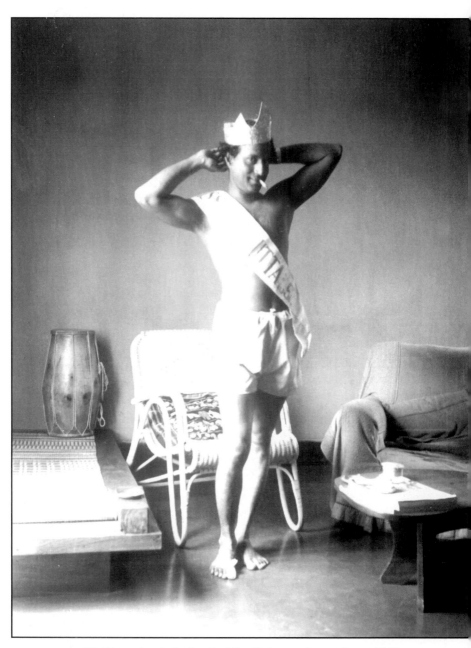

Habib posing in Indrani's Miss Calcutta decorations, 1952

Habib & Indrani, Juhu Beach, Bombay
Photo: Rama Chattopadhyaya

Ramlal Bajpai welcoming daughter
Indrani to New York, 1952

G. Venkatachalam, Indrani & Harin, Constitution House, New Delhi, 1953

*Ragini Devi as Parvati in the dance
'Parvati Lasya Sringara Nritya'*

Guru Sikkil Ramaswamy Pillai & Indrani

Indrani, Sukanya, Balu Bhagvatar, unknown, E. Krishna Iyer,
Rang Vittal & Ritha Chatterji, Melatur, 1953
Photo: Courtesy Rang Vittal

Sukanya & Indrani pulling water from a well, Melatur, 1953
Photo: Rang Vittal

Sukanya, 1953
Photo: Rang Vittal

(Right)
Indrani, Melatur,
1953
Photo: Courtesy Rang Vittal

(Below) Ramlal
Bajpai & Sukanya,
Delhi, 1954
Photo: Habib Rahman

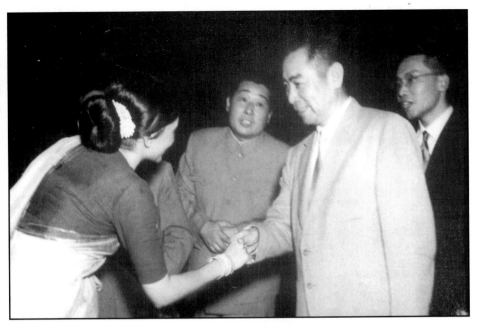

Indrani with Chou En-lai, New Delhi, 1955

Indrani, J.F. Kennedy, Mrs. Jackie Kennedy, Nehru, Rose Kennedy
& Ambassador B.K. Nehru, Washington D.C., 1961

Photo: UPI

(Left)
Indrani, Ted Shawn, Martha Graham
at Jacob's Pillow, 1960
Photo: Courtesy John Lindquist

(Below)
Indrani & Sukanya on a tour of
Hong Kong & Malaysia, 1965

Sukanya in Odissi
Photo: Habib Rahman

(Above)
Frank Wicks, Sukanya,
Wardreath, Habib,
Ragini, Indrani
& Ram, Actors' Fund
Home, New Jersey,
1978

(Right)
Sukanya playing
tanpura for Indrani,
Scala Theatre, London,
1967

*Kamala Devi Chattopadhyaya, Chairperson, Sangeet Natak Akademi, presenting
a scroll honouring Ragini Devi (posthumously) to Indrani, 1982*

Sukanya, Ragini & Indrani
Three generations' performance, New York University Theatre, 29 September 1979
Photo: Ram Rahman

(Right)
Indrani in Odissi
at Filmore East,
New York, 1968
Photo: Ivan Spane

(Below)
Indrani in Odissi with
Srinivasa Murthy
& Deva Prasad Das

Mulk Raj Anand, Indrani, Deva Prasad Das & Dr. Mansingh

(Above)
Charles, Venka, etc.,
at Sujan Singh Park,
New Delhi

(Right)
Ragini Devi & Vallathol
at Kalamandalam

Ram/Oscar in a pose
Photo: Habib Rahman

*Chokkalingam Pillai, Meenakshisundaram Pillai,
Muthiah Pillai, Ritha Chatterji, Sukanya, Indrani
in Pandanallur, 1953*

the Natanam Adinar, I would sit mesmerised, and try to memorise each step and gesture and words to the song sung in the melodious raga, Ananda Bhairavi, and set to a lively rhythm of fourteen beats.

From the first stamp of the dance to the last she ceased being my mother. Her flashing eyes, her eyebrows, her fingers, her arms, her raised foot, her entire being, vividly brought to life the image of the four-armed Shiva Nataraja, King of Dancers, performing his awesome cosmic dance. Serpents twisted around his arms and neck swayed as he danced, his matted locks swayed, the earth heaved, the waters of the sacred Ganga splashed.

The same dishevelled, mystical Shiva, portrayed as lover and consort of Parvati in the interminably long varnams, failed to sustain my interest for long. Passages of rhythmic dance interspersing the poetic passages relieved some of the monotony.

Variations of gesture and mime that could illuminate a single line of poetry were endless. It was not enough to beg Shiva not to reject his beloved at the twilight hour. Parted from Shiva, Parvati could take no pleasure in eating. She wasted away, her sleep disturbed by dreams of Shiva. She could not bear to hear the nightingales sing. Silvery beams of the full moon scorched her eyes.

My attention span was limited. Twenty minutes into the dance I'd start squirming and fidgeting. Parvati's expressions of ecstasy would turn into Shiva's third eye flashing daggers at me. My mother would lose her concentration, and Chokkalingam's stick would crack over her shin.

There was no Ayah to whisk me out of the room at the first signs of restlessness. Madras was dredged for people willing to take me off my mother's hands and out from under her stomping feet. One unforgettable volunteer was Dr. Sarangapani Ayyangar, a Sanskrit scholar, benefactor of the Institute of Fine Arts and an advocate of the Supreme Court of India. He was a wiry, soft-spoken orthodox Brahmin. Under his turban a tuft of hair sprouted from an otherwise cleanly shaven head, and swung down to the back of his neck. He wore the advocates' funereal black jacket, and shoes with socks held up by a pair of Paris Garters, visible under his dhoti when he walked.

Shoes were removed before entering his home, which was kept spotless by his plump wife and two pretty daughters of marriageable age. They'd concoct ingenious schemes to keep me occupied. They sang and danced for me, and taught me a simple South Indian folk dance, with Tamil words to the accompanying song. They showed me how to play Jacks with little stones. They fed me spicy vadas and steamed idlis. We drank strong hot coffee out of stainless-steel mugs. (Yet when Sarangapani visited our home in Delhi he refused all food and drink. It seems that touching utensils in the home of my Muslim father would defile him for life.)

These tasty, carefree times in Sarangapani's home ended when Chokkalingam consented to take me on as a pupil.

We had to wait for the proper conjunction of planets before he could start teaching me. When the auspicious day arrived I placed at his feet the customary offering of betel leaves, bananas, coconut, incense, a white cotton angavastra with a gold border, some coins of silver, and his fees, discreetly placed in an envelope.

When Mummy first mentioned she might have to take me along on her next dance study trip to South India, I had fantasies of learning the Natanam Adinar from her guru, and getting into costume and make-up and performing before an audience. I was confident the basic adavus my grandmother had taken such pains to teach me in Bangalore were sufficient for performing an entire dance.

But no.

"Tei ya tei—tei ya tei—tei ya tei."

For hours, for days, for weeks on end, I stamped my feet and repeated the same steps of Bharata Natyam Nani had already drilled into me.

"No one should walk out of this class," Chokkalingam hollered in Tamil, when I complained of sore feet and aching muscles. "They should be carried out on stretchers and taken to the hospital!"

The hour and a half of torture was dished out to me at the end of my mother's class—though what was torture to me seemed pure ecstasy to her.

There was, blissfully, relief in sight.

My grandmother had for some time been prodding my mother to travel to the village of Melatur to investigate the Bhagavata Mela Natakam, a fast-dying form of dance drama performed once a year during the week-long festivities honouring Narasimha, man-lion avatar of Vishnu.

E. Krishna Iyer, early champion of Bharata Natyam, arranged for our stay and travel to the village of Melatur. Included in our excursion besides Iyer, my mother and myself, were three other dance enthusiasts: Robert Riviera, an American student of Bharata Natyam who had changed his name to Nala Najan; Ritha Chatterji, a Manipuri dancer; and Rang Vittal, a Kathak dancer.

Our train journey as far as the town of Kumbhakonam was uneventful. When the train made a stop in Kumbhakonam, one of the dancers dashed into a nearby souvenir shop and purchased a four-foot high, gaudy brass image of the dancing Shiva Nataraja.

We got off the train at Ayyampet station, and after refreshing ourselves on the juice and creamy meat of tender green coconuts, we all squeezed into a covered bullock cart for the remaining four-mile ride to the village of Melatur. To keep from rolling off the back of the cart I clung tightly to Nataraja. Each time our team of bullocks took us over a rut, the four-armed God of Dance reminded me of his destructive powers with a bloody jab of the jagged flames of his cosmic ring. I was secretly relieved when the wheels of our decrepit cart settled into the muddy bed of a river. Nataraja remained in the cart, while the rest of us removed our sandals, hitched up our saris, dhotis and skirts and waded across the river to wait while villagers pushed the cart across the river.

Our two bullocks lumbered into Melatur at dusk and deposited us in front of the Varadaraj Perumal temple that housed the image of Narasimha. The temple, a modest miniature version of the towering richly carved gopurams typical of Tamil Nadu, was flanked by two simple domes and surrounded by a high wall, freshly painted in auspicious red and white stripes. Besides the temple, Melatur consisted of three unpaved streets. Two rows of houses in front of the temple belonged to the Bhagavatas—the Brahmin actor-dancers whose ancestors had, according to legend, been deeded the land by

king Achyutappa (A.D. 1572–1614) to propagate their art and enhance
the spirit of Bhakti, devotion. Each year the Bhagavatas, who were
forced to seek a livelihood in distant towns, returned to perform
in the dance dramas.

The air, fanned by swaying coconut palms, was sweet, especially
after malodorous Madras, the streets swept clean. The entire village
wore a festive look. Doorways to each home were strung with
garlands of mango leaves; floors were decorated with intricate
patterns of rangoli. We were led to a single-storey house quite close
to the temple, and seemingly as ancient. The house had a sloping
terracotta-tiled roof, and sparsely furnished rooms surrounding a
central courtyard with a well. It seemed emptied of its occupants,
yet Ritha, my mother and I were put in one room, lit only with
kerosene lamps. Soon after putting down our bags we were invited
to join other members of our group in a neighbouring house.

A sumptuous vegetarian dinner, consisting primarily of an
enormous mountain of rice, sambar, vegetables and yogurt, was
served to us on large banana leaves by a matronly Brahmin lady who
had a massive diamond dripping from her nostril. She wore her sari
South Indian style, with no front pleats and hitched up through the
back of her legs. We sat cross-legged on white sheets spread over
the floor, and ate with our fingers. Following our hosts' example, we
doused out the fire with water glugged from stainless steel tumblers
without putting our lips to the edges.

All through the night large creatures, which I thought were cats,
scurried over us as we tried to sleep on the thin straw matting on
the floor. When we mentioned this to E. Krishna Iyer next morning
he informed us matter-of-factly that our nocturnal visitors were
actually bandicoots—overgrown rats.

Besides the famous dance drama which was to be held at night,
there was nothing much to see in the village. This was just as well,
since our entire morning was taken up with our ablutions. I was
trying to catch up on lost sleep when I heard shrieks coming from
the direction of the courtyard. I thought perhaps it was my mother
who had mysteriously vanished, so I ran out to the courtyard with
all the heroism I could muster. Ritha, partially clothed and covered

with soap-suds, looking like some damsel in a Ravi Verma painting, was trembling beside the well and timidly throwing mugfuls of water at a large buffalo that had sauntered in—evidently with no ill intentions.

Meanwhile my mother was still missing. I peered into the lush green fields behind the house, but all I could see was an outhouse covered with palm fronds and some goats grazing nearby. One goat was nibbling through the wall of the latrine. Through this newly constructed window I spotted my mother's eyes, wide as saucers and frozen in terror.

Before a badly needed afternoon nap she volunteered to give me a brief synopsis of the story of *Prahalada Charitram*, the drama we were to see later that night. This story revolved around young Prahalada, devotee of the god Vishnu, and his demonic father Hiranyakashipu who, after undergoing severe penance, had been granted a boon of immortality from Brahma. He could be killed neither by day nor by night, by neither man nor beast, neither indoors nor outdoors. Jealous of his son's devotion to Vishnu, the invincible Hiranyakashipu challenged the god to manifest himself. Vishnu, assuming his man-lion avatar Narasimha, leapt out of a pillar. The half-man half-beast carried Hiranyakashipu to the threshold, and at dusk destroyed the evil father by disembowelling him.

The story, in the comparative safety of our room, was no scarier than a typical fairy tale. But I was not prepared for the drama that unfolded on that starry summer night. An improvised stage, erected in front of the temple at audience level, was lit only by the eerie glow of earthen oil lamps set on banana-tree trunks. After a puja to Ganesh was performed, E. Krishna Iyer was invited to inaugurate the festival and give a speech. The dance drama opened with the entrance of a buffoon who, with his pranks and jokes, immediately grabbed the attention of the noisily excited audience. Suddenly the drama took on a more austere aspect with individual introductions of the cast of characters who made their entrances from behind a satin patchwork curtain carried by two stagehands dressed in dhotis.

The all-male cast costumed in slightly frayed brocade saris, velvet robes, oversized moustaches, wooden ornaments and crowns covered in gold paper and mirror, danced and sang, recited verse, conversed with each other and addressed the audience, using exaggerated gestures and melodramatic dialogue. As the drama progressed some characters seemed possessed by the very gods, demigods and demons they were portraying.

I nodded off during long passages of Telugu dialogue I could not follow, but I'm certain I was not dreaming when two attendants of the evil Hiranyakashipu actually frothed at the mouth in their frenzy. Towards the end of the night a terrifying, brilliantly masked Narasimha leapt out from behind a pillar to confront Hiranyakashipu; he was in such a deep trance that two stagehands had to restrain him with a long scarf tied around his middle. I hid behind the palloo of Mummy's sari, hoping to miss the gory finale. But the demon's death was, mercifully, only referred to symbolically.

The play ended with the rapidly breaking dawn. While the Bhagavatas sang an early-morning raga, the actors, still in costume, walked through the audience and circumambulated the deity in the temple. Villagers showered the masked Narasimha with flower petals, and waved an oil lamp and performed arati before him. Then the actors paraded through the streets to the accompaniment of drums, cymbals, chants, the nasal whine of the clarinet-like nadaswaram and the blowing of the conch, receiving from each house gratitude, honour and a sprinkling of rose water.

Next evening a seminar was held comparing various styles of classical dance. Ritha Chatterji demonstrated Manipuri from the northeastern part of India, my mother danced a few items of Bharata Natyam, Rang Vittal presented a sampling of Kathak, and Nala Najan danced a tillana he had choreographed on the spot.

Feeling a little left out, I stood before the distinguished gathering and announced that I, too, was going to dance. My mother, shocked at my brazen behavior, called me back. But before she could drag me off, E. Krishna Iyer jumped up and asked what I wanted to dance. Natanam Adinar, I told him. I forced my mother into singing for me while I imitated all the familiar and well-memorised poses and movements and rhythms. When it was over, the seniormost artist, Balu Bhagvatar, comforted my mother: "This baby is going to be a great dancer. I am surprised at her courage to face the audience without the least fear."

I was in another world, and quite oblivious to the audience. With this dance of bliss, those tortuous hours of stamping feet dissolved into ecstasy.

I had mortified my mother by my lack of modesty. But Shiva Nataraja didn't seem to mind. In fact I'm certain he had been appeased by my performance, since he refrained from inflicting any more wounds on me during our trip back to Madras.

14

Cultural Goodwill

The downside of my mother's rising fame in the dance world was her frequent absence from home; the upside was the decidedly global ambience that was now infused into our daily lives. Ulan Bator, Sinkiang, Bucharest, Yerevan were no longer merely place names in the atlas but places from where we received postcards, letters and gifts.

Conquering the world with dance was almost as grand a passion for her as performing. The day she received a phone call from the Ministry of Culture inviting her to participate in a tour to China, Mummy went berserk with excitement and came perilously close to losing her life. To celebrate this forthcoming tour, and perhaps to soften the blow of yet another spell away from home, she offered to treat me to a Chinese lunch at Nirula's in Connaught Place. On our way to the restaurant, driving along Curzon Road in a four-seater autorickshaw, she noticed her good friend, writer and dance critic V.V. Prasad, riding on a scooter in the opposite direction.

"V.V., I'm going to dance in China! I'm going to dance in China!" she leaned out and screamed across the street to him, practically falling overboard as she waved her arms trying to catch his attention. Luckily one of our fellow passengers held onto her, snatching back the palloo of her fluttering magenta silk sari seconds before it was sucked into the spokes of the auto's wheels.

Her enthusiasm turned out to be justified, since the Chinese government rolled out the red carpet for the troupe of artists from India and showered them with lavish hospitality. The Goverment of India cultural delegation included samplings of dance and music from every part of India—the great Hindustani vocalist D.V. Paluskar, sitarist Abdul Haleem Jaffar Khan, a troupe of Manipuri dancers, Kathakali dance drama, the not-so-little Little Ballet Troupe which enacted fables from the *Panchatantra*, Kathak dancers, folk singers from Bengal, strapping Sikh Bhangra dancers from Punjab, and Bharata Natyam performed by Indrani.

The opening performance in Beijing was attended by Mao Zedong, Chou En-lai and their visitor from North Vietnam, Ho Chi Minh, who, according to reports in the press, unbuttoned his Mandarin-collared jacket down to his undershirt and applauded heartily all through the programme. The evening ended on a delectably high note with Chou En-lai hosting a traditional Chinese banquet for the delegation of artistes.

We had by then shifted from our temporary lodgings at Constitution House to a more spacious flat that my father had been assigned by the government. Soon after Mummy's return home from the two-month long tour, the drawing room of our new flat in Sujan Singh Park began to resemble a Chinese curio shop. Indian handloom cushions and bedspreads were replaced by brilliantly coloured silks embroidered with dragons, chrysanthemums and peonies; a carved wooden lamp with painted glass panels and red tassels, was placed on top of an ornate rosewood table. Daddy had one of his carpenters construct a special glass case to display miniature clay masks representing characters from the Beijing Opera. The walls were plastered with Chinese ink drawings of horses, wispy water colours of coniferous trees and ethereal mountains veiled in swirls of mist, photographic silk portraits of Chairman Mao alongside portraits of my mother's new heart-throb, Chou En-lai.

Her wardrobe changed as well. She now lounged lazily about the flat in a wine-red silk quilted jacket. Her dangly silver earrings and jade necklace with the image of Kuan Yin, Goddess of Mercy, blended in harmoniously with the rest of the decor.

Practically each day red silk invitations embossed in gold arrived from the Chinese embassy, as did diplomats from the embassy who came bearing gifts of jasmine tea, dried lichees, and giant ornamental cabbages and chrysanthemums from their gardens. Happily, I was often included in their invitations to teas and cocktail receptions held on the lawns of the embassy situated in the old Jind House on Lytton Road. The social scene didn't particularly interest me—I was, in fact, painfully shy and tongue-tied, but all shyness vanished when it came to the succulent food, which, unlike Delhi's Chinese restaurants, was fine and delicate, and exquisitely served, with mouth-watering soups ladled out of virtually translucent winter melons. One of the diplomat's wives went out of her way to teach me how to wield a pair of long ivory chopsticks. I also learned to swim in the Olympic-sized embassy pool and shared with the embassy children the gigantic yellow "Happy Hippo" inflatable tube my mother had brought me from China.

Those were the days of "Hindi-Chini Bhai Bhai": Indo-Chinese brotherhood and friendship. The slogan was borrowed from a song composed by our old friend Harin Chattopadhyaya. When it was sung right after the Indian national anthem by the Indian delegation in China, some Members of Parliament back in Delhi had protested, calling it filthy communist propaganda. Prime Minister Nehru refused to heed rumours circulating about the capital that his Chinese brothers were amassing troops along the borders of Tibet.

The Delhi Gymkhana Club, a staid relic of the British Raj where members (now mostly Indian) of the private club could play the pucca burra sahib, was the unlikely venue of an official government reception that cemented this brotherhood.

Often the setting for ballroom dances and children's fancy dress parties, the main hall was, on that particular evening, taken over by Prime Minister Nehru who was playing host to a trio of dignitaries from China and Tibet. This cavernous room in the central building of the club was filling up fast with the usual assortment of characters who turned up at every official or diplomatic function in the city: foreign ambassadors who arrived in chauffeur-driven cars with their countries' flags fluttering proudly, bureaucrats, joint secretaries, under secretaries and other Indian government officials dressed in stiff high-collared tunics, glamorous socialites in gorgeous saris, and a faithful flock of impoverished artists and journalists who depended on these affairs for their daily intake of food, drink and gossip.

My parents were by now accustomed to carting me along to these functions. I was almost nine, and to them it was perhaps preferable to enduring my constant complaints of boredom and tantrums on being left alone with Ayah and Abdul, the servant Dadi had sent from Calcutta to replace Johnny. For this occasion my mother was outfitted in her Chinese finery: a long black and gold brocade cape over her silk sari. When Panditji, ever chivalrous to beautiful women, spotted her, he grabbed her by the elbow and whisked her off to meet the dignitaries. I followed, nervously clutching onto my mother's cape.

The chief guest turned out to be a tall, striking, bushy-browed Chinese gentleman who strongly resembled one of the portraits decorating our drawing room wall. I could practically hear Mummy's heart explode as Chou En-lai leaned down to her and graciously mumbled something about recalling his meeting her in Beijing and seeing her dance. Standing on either side of the Chinese premier were two young Tibetan monks who, my mother later whispered to me, were the Dalai Lama and the Panchen Lama. Their heads were shaved and they were dressed in sleeveless maroon robes and canvas sneakers.

The dignitaries spoke little but smiled serenely throughout the evening. No one on that glittery occasion could possibly have imagined that the Chinese were conspiring to invade India, nor could anyone have predicted the seemingly benign Dalai Lama was plotting to flee Tibet and seek asylum in India.

Unaware history was in the making around me, I was more in awe of the avuncular Nehru than his important guests. Before I could muster up the nerve to tell him we shared the same birthday, crowds of well-wishers began pressing in to get close to the VIPs. I let go of my mother's Chinese cape and wandered off in pursuit of a smartly turbaned bearer, passing around a tray filled with drinks, and discreetly helped myself to a glass of sweet sherry. The remainder of the evening was one happy blur.

My mother had not elected to wear that cape for merely decorative purposes: it ingeniously concealed what had remained a family secret for the duration of the China tour. Lurking somewhere under the folds of the voluminous cape was Oscar.

Necessitated by a fear of being dropped from the cultural delegation, "Oscar" was the code name for a most inconveniently-timed pregnancy.

When my brother was born on the morning of 16 November 1955, he was officially given the name Ram, after Ramlal Bajpai. That name, much to his consternation in later years, was seldom used. The code name Oscar stuck like yet another memento from China.

Oscar was a red, shrivelled up creature who winked continuously as he surveyed the world from my mother's arms. All he owned in the way of clothing was the towel in which the Tirath Ram hospital had bundled him up. Although her mother-in-law was miles away in Calcutta, Mummy had not dared run the risk of making any preparations for Oscar's arrival in deference to Dadi's superstition. As a result Daddy, Ayah and I found ourselves staying up late into that first night of his life, cutting up squares of pastel-coloured Binney's flannel and stitching them up into sack-like gowns.

Oscar, nine years my junior, began to interest me only after he was old enough to take the unpopular roles of old ladies and servants in the variety shows my Sujan Singh Park friends and I would mount every so often. The dining room was our stage while the audience sat in the drawing room. Our performances were really an extension of dressing up in costumes pulled out of my grandmother's old trunk which now, covered with a piece of striped silk from Kashgar, doubled as the telephone table.

This trunk was bursting with jewelled wooden headdresses, a slinky black net cobra costume covered in silver sequins, black tresses made out of straw, long silver finger nails, mirrored and embroidered skirts and backless cholis which were slightly moth-eaten and smelt of decades of stale sweat, and yards and yards of beads and bangles and earrings that required patient untangling before they could be worn.

The themes and stories of our variously-costumed skits and dance dramas were dictated by the contents of the trunk. My father rigged up the lighting and my mother donated the make-up.

We ran door-to-door coercing grown-ups to purchase tickets and patiently endure our performances, and later blew our profits on Coca-Colas at the Empire Store in Khan Market. But these home-brewed performances turned out to be my stepping stone to the real thing.

Often during my mother's performances her musical accompanists would allow me to sit beside them, just close enough to the stage to get a good view of the dancing and the audience. One memorable night, prior to a performance she was giving at a music conference in Banaras, I was recruited to assist backstage. It was my job to make sure no one would disturb Mummy while she prepared for the performance.

The transition from everyday face to stage face was a tricky one. One ill-timed knock on the greenroom door while she applied her elaborate eye make-up could break her concentration and put her in a foul mood for the rest of the evening. She had a set of pre-performance rituals which seldom varied. I watched as she methodically draped her costumes over a chair in the order of items on the programme. Then she laid out her ornaments and cosmetics on the dresser, and placed her ankle bells and some dried rose petals in front of an image of Ganesh. Just before starting her make-up she stuck several sticks of Mysore sandalwood incense into an empty miniature bottle of Rémy Martin and lit them with a match—both bottle and matches, mementos from tours abroad, were of sentimental value. And then, as if in a trance, she waved the slowly uncurling, delicately scented smoke, over costumes, jewels, and ankle bells before leaving the sticks to burn in front of Ganesh, the auspicious elephant-headed god who removes obstacles and is worshipped by artistes before each performance.

It was my responsibility as well to ward off strangers seeking autographs, free passes and photographs. Alas, what transpired during the Banaras performance was beyond my control. Right in the middle of a physically and mentally demanding varnam, an overly ambitious press-photographer leaped up on stage, stood between my mother and the audience and began to snap away. My mother stopped dancing, silenced the musicians with the palm of one hand, raised an eyebrow to heaven, spewed out the most effective American expletives in her vocabulary, then grabbed the fellow by his collar and dragged him into the wings. Reliable sources later reported that the petrified photographer headed straight for the railway station and jumped on the first train out of Banaras—presumably in search of a new profession.

This unfortunate incident was not held against me. In fact my stage duties soon extended to playing the tanpura, an easily strummed, long-necked gourd instrument whose four strings provide the hypnotic drone essential to Indian music.

One hard-to-forget evening in November 1956 my musical and backstage duties almost came to an ignoble end. Mummy had been invited by Nehru to dance before Emperor Haile Selassie of Ethiopia. Each dignitary's visit to Delhi included a formal state banquet followed by a cultural programme in the grand ballroom of Rashtrapati Bhavan, former viceregal lodge and now India's presidential palace.

Since security was tight, there were no unsavoury characters for me to fend off. It was my first time inside Rashtrapati Bhavan, so I took advantage of the few moments before the "house" opened to admire Sir Edwin Lutyens' architectural masterpiece. I strolled onto the makeshift stage and with my mouth wide open and my head up to the ceiling, gaped at the fine crystal chandeliers, gilded moldings and frescoes on the high ceiling. Suddenly there was an ear-shattering explosion with glass flying all over—then darkness.

I had inadvertently walked right into the long set of footlights and tripped over them. When the President's bodyguards, dressed in crisp red tunics and gold and white turbans, leapt out of nowhere to supervise the clean up and removal of glass from the VIPs' front-row sofas, I was certain they had come with orders to haul me off and lock me up in the palace dungeons.

To my astonishment and relief there was, instead, genuine concern as to whether I had been hurt. But aside from wounded pride, I was unscathed. Moments before the Imperial entourage, led by the President of India Dr. Rajendra Prasad, Pandit Nehru, Indira Gandhi and Sardar Patel, were to make their entrance into the ballroom, several standard floodlights were hastily plugged in and the show went on.

The soothing strains of the opening alaap, performed by an instrumental trio from All India Radio who were sharing the programme, soon smoothed out many frayed nerves. Nehru sank comfortably into the sofa, his chin dropped to his chest as he launched contentedly into his legendary post-banquet snore, blissfully ignorant of the little drama that had preceded his entrance.

I was relieved my clumsiness had not marred my mother's performance. It might have actually enhanced it, since there was more cosmic fire than usual in her Natanam Adinar, the dance in praise of Shiva. In her signature piece, Sariga Kongu, as the mischievous child-god Krishna, she offered Haile Selassie and Nehru (who had been nudged awake by his daughter) balls of butter which she then teasingly popped into her own mouth. A foot-stomping, fast-paced, intricately patterned tillana ended the programme and brought the notoriously restrained audience of bureaucrats to life with their applause.

Instead of leading Haile Selassie on stage to greet the artistes, as was his custom, Nehru shouted to my mother to step down into the audience. The diminutive Emperor of Ethiopia, with his frizzy beard and elongated head, bowed stiffly before my mother and put into her hands some Ethiopian gold coins. Standing next to the Emperor was his tall, regal-looking daughter who was wearing a heavy silver belt with a gold crest. He whispered something to her. She immediately removed the belt which her father then handed over to my mother.

The Emperor's lavish gifts momentarily eclipsed her memory of happenings earlier in the evening. However, a respectable period of time elapsed before my next encounter with any international royalty or heads of state at Rashtrapati Bhavan. Someone else was assigned to play the tanpura when my mother danced for the US President, Dwight Eisenhower, but when she danced for Queen Elizabeth II and the Duke of Edinburgh, and later Richard and Pat Nixon, I was recruited back into the troupe and my conduct was impeccable.

15

Puri Pilgrimage

aile Selassie's gold coins and silver belt went into my father's closet for safekeeping, which usually meant we would never see them again. The Pharaoh's Tomb, as my mother referred to this hallowed repository, was a veritable duty-free shop. Interred in the camphor-scented tomb with Daddy's suits and overcoats from America were his cameras, rolls of film, jumbo bottles of Scotch whisky, French cognacs, liqueurs, jars of imported olives, tins of tuna fish, packets of Knorr Soup, Swiss chocolates, and a wind-up monkey that played cymbals and danced in circles. This toy was a "look but don't touch" gift that my parents had brought back for me from Tokyo during their Pan American world tour.

But the Emperor's belt wasn't destined to remain entombed for long.

For many years Ragini had been talking about a form of dance that existed in Orissa based on the rules of the *Natya Shastra* and descended from the style referred to there as the dance of "Odra Desa," ancient name of Orissa. She was certain the dance was still being performed by temple dancers in the temple of Jagannath in Puri as part of the daily rituals, but she did not know its name. She believed this dance was one of the most perfect classical systems of dance still surviving in India.

She urged my mother to go to Orissa to investigate these dances and report on whether this dance was classical or not, and if it turned out to be what she thought it was, to master it. To Ragini's regret her own preoccupation with Kathakali and Bharata Natyam, in the early years, had left her little time or energy to seriously pursue other dance forms. My mother was busy as well back then with her own studies of Bharata Natyam. But after years of performing Bharata Natyam she was restless to enrich her repertoire with other forms. She had returned to Kalamandalam as the guest of Vallathol and his wife and studied Mohini Attam, and Ragini had passed on to her the Kuchipudi "Dasavatara," which she herself had learned from a great old Kuchipudi guru. Then at last she heard something more definite about the Orissan dance form, "Orissi" or "Odissi."

Delhi audiences were offered a brief glimpse of this dance style during an inter-university youth festival at Talkatora Gardens, when a young biology student from Orissa, Priyambada Mohanty, performed at the open-air theatre. My mother was away touring in Europe, but Charles Fabri insisted Daddy and I accompany him to the performance. My father, being aware of my mother's interest in this dance form kept a cutting of Fabri's review. On her return she asked Fabri for details of the dance form. He assured her that Odissi was a beautiful and graceful classical form of dance and encouraged her to study it, feeling it would suit her well.

Through Fabri's intervention, negotiations for my mother to investigate this dance form were set in motion. She bombarded his friends and colleagues in Orissa with letters asking for help in witnessing the dance in its place of origin, and in finding a guru who would teach her. There was hesitation at first; some of those she contacted expressed embarrassment at her seeing Odissi, feeling she might regard it as folk dance as compared to classical Bharata

Natyam. Finally Fabri's good friend, Dr. Mayadhar Mansinh, gave in to her volley of letters and invited her to attend a seminar on Odissi dance, held by the Utkal Nritya Sangeet Natyakala Parishad.

In the May of 1957, when Delhi turned into its habitual furnace and most cultural activities sizzled to a halt, my mother and I boarded a train headed for Puri, one of India's holiest cities. I was thrilled to be included in this expedition, but after our Melatur experience I was somewhat apprehensive and prepared myself for all forms of jungle life. What a delightful surprise, then, to be received at the railway station by an official welcoming committee and driven by car to the Bengal Northern Railway hotel, the BNR, where Mummy and I were to be guests of the government of Orissa.

A sweeping veranda, furnished with wicker chairs, potted palms and floor fans lazily humming, ran the length of the old colonial resort overlooking the Bay of Bengal. Carved out of ice and illuminated with rainbow lights, a graceful swan dominated the high-ceilinged dining room which served both Indian and Continental cuisine. A sign on the wall reminded guests that quiet hours were between 10 p.m. to 6 a.m. and 2 p.m. to 4 p.m.

Word of the renowned Bharata Natyam dancer's arrival and her interest in Odissi had spread faster than the Mahanadi in flood. A stream of Odissi gurus from around the state, all hoping to be selected as her teacher, descended on the hotel; uniformed bearers balancing trays of tea wound their way through the corridors, now overrun with dhoti-clad dance masters. The gurus presented their credentials and begged my mother to come and visit their schools and see their students perform.

Since this trip coincided with the symposium on Odissi dance, each evening I tagged along with my mother to see the performances, mostly in the form of dance dramas presented in an institutional auditorium in conjunction with talks and lectures. The lovely Priyambada Mohanty danced alongwith Sanjukta Panigrahi and Mayadhar Raut who had recently returned from studying Bharata Natyam at Kalakshetra.

Some of the dancers performing were very young girls with elastic joints who wove into their dance astonishing acrobatic feats. Their faces were decorated with little dots of sandalwood paste, painted above their eyebrows and snaking down the cheeks. Spiked flowers, crafted out of pith, encircled their elaborately coiffed hair. The costuming verged on tacky and gaudy: brightly coloured South Indian silk dhotis, topped by velvet blouses encrusted with imitation gems. Draped over the blouses and tied around the waist were gossamer Banarasi scarves. The girls were decked from head to toe with silver filigree jewellry from Orissa and gold ornaments studded with imitation pearls and rubies from South India.

Despite the elaborate packaging the dancers sank effortlessly into deep pliés with feet set wide apart, slim arms wove circles around their heads, their weight shifted lusciously in and out of a Tribhangi with the hip thrust to one side, shoulder thrust opposite, the head tilted in the direction of swinging hips. One dancer, resting on her belly, began circling the floor; her hands, raised above her head and holding on to her feet, formed a perfect wheel. I was ten years old and no connoisseur, but the dancers' fluid movements set to the gentle beat of the drum and the sweet notes of the flute appealed to me more than the more-familiar Bharata Natyam which suddenly seemed austere and sharp-edged in comparison.

When we weren't admiring dancers on stage, we were admiring dancers frozen in time, carved into myriad Orissan temples dating from the seventh century A.D.

An eminent scholar of Carnatic music, who was attending the seminar with his wife, joined us one morning for an excursion to Konarak, the thirteenth-century temple dedicated to Surya, the Sun God. A good part of the road between Puri and Konarak simply did not exist, so it was no surprise when the ancient Dodge station-wagon we were riding in skidded on the sand dunes and gently settled on its side. We were all unhurt and managed to crawl out of the car and keep relatively calm . . . all except our scholar. According to his calculations we were right in the middle of Rahu Kaalam, an adverse time, especially for travel. He settled down in the shade of a cashew tree, removed his turban, and anxiously fanned himself with one end of the cotton and gold-bordered angavastra draped around his neck, biding out the inauspicious conjunction of planets. Meanwhile his comfortably plump wife hitched up her kanjeevaram silk sari and joined the rest of us in digging the car out of the hot sand with our bare hands.

The Sun God and the granite serenity of Konarak obliterated the negative aspects of Rahu Kaalam. This splendid temple, shaped in the form of a chariot, was set on twenty-four ornately carved wheels drawn by seven straining horses. I clung close to my mother as we circumambulated the Black Pagoda and climbed dizzying heights to admire life-sized figures of voluptuous dancers and musicians precariously perched along the ledges of the spire. More challenging to admire, especially in the presence of grown-ups, were graphic friezes of intimately entwined couples carved into the base of the chariot and the walls and pillars of the ruins of the Nata Mandap, the dance hall. I ultimately resorted to examining my feet or staring at the sky at critical moments, since all the temples were similarly embellished.

Just minutes away from the sterile civility of the BNR hotel existed an entirely different India: noisy narrow lanes, bazaars exuding pungent odours, throngs of pilgrims laden with offerings of fruits, sweets and flowers, jamming the entrances to the great temple of Jagannath.

Fervent Hindus believed that pilgrims who stayed three days and three nights in Puri would obtain release from the eternal cycle of birth and rebirth. I ventured anonymously into both the Jagannath temple at Puri and the Lingaraja temple at Bhuvaneshwar without my mother. Pictures of her, with the last name Rahman, on the front pages of the daily papers, identified her as the wife of a Muslim. As these temples were still religiously active, entry was forbidden to all non-Hindus. Non-Hindus and foreigners were, however, welcome to view the courtyard of the temple from the gallery of a neighbouring rooftop. Mummy balked at offers to have a glimpse of the temple from the foreigners' gallery. I couldn't help feeling embarrassed when she informed our kind, puzzled hosts, with some disdain, that as the daughter of a high-caste Bajpai Brahmin she could not stoop to such indignity.

Happily the ceremonial Chandan Yatra, which took place outside the temple, was free of such restrictions and could be enjoyed by

Hindus and non-Hindus alike. Once a year the image of the god Jagannath, an incarnation of Krishna-Vishnu, was taken in procession to a tank three miles away and placed on a boat. The boat floated around in chandan (sandalwood) scented water while Maharis (temple dancers) and Gotipuas (boy-dancers), in two accompanying boats, entertained the deity with song and dance.

Viewing the temple dancers from a distance was not entirely sufficient for my mother. Her numerous requests to be taken to the home of a Mahari were met with silence. A ladies' tea was arranged instead at the governor of Puri's seaside mansion where, she was informed, she would have an opportunity to meet a genuine Mahari.

It was hardly a meeting. In the midst of all the chatter and clatter of cups and spoons there was a sudden hush. Standing in the doorway of the grand drawing room was a young woman dressed in a plain cotton sari, her head covered discreetly. My mother, suspecting who it might be, rushed up to the temple dancer and tried to invite her in for a cup of tea. There was a clearing of throats and an awkward exchange of looks between the ladies, who were clearly unprepared for the reality of allowing someone they considered a concubine and prostitute into their midst. I couldn't comprehend all the fuss and concentrated on the sweets on my plate, but the poor woman, clearly aware of her position, remained standing by the door.

Some days later, while I was left in the care of some fishermen on the beach, my mother was taken by cycle-rickshaw to the red-light district of Puri where the Maharis lived. Deva Prasad Das, the Odissi guru she had chosen to study with, had offered to escort her to see the Maharis perform in their home. They performed daily in the sanctum of the Jagannath temple but these performances were part of ancient temple ritual, not for public viewing. A local Raja, himself quite penniless as a result of revocation of privy purses by the Indian government, was paying the Maharis five rupees a month to continue the ritual ceremonies at the Jagannath temple.

The leading dancer, who let them into her modest single-storeyed dwelling, had, at first, been afraid to perform. Hoping to break out of her destined profession, she was studying to become a nurse. If word got around she was from a caste of concubines she would be thrown out of nursing school.

Despite their initial hesitation the women danced excerpts from the *Gita Govinda*, the only dances performed in the temple. My mother was moved by the beauty of their dancing but was saddened at their plight. They requested her to put her opinion of their art in writing. The certificates she wrote out stated that their art was an ancient classical and highly aesthetic dance which should be revived and subsidised by the state government of Orissa, and supported by those people of Orissa who respect the arts. Some years later she found out from Deva Prasad Das that these same Maharis had opened schools of dance and with copies of their precious testimonials tacked up on the walls began taking in students from respectable Oriya families.

My mother was impatient to start studying Odissi right away with Guru Deva Prasad Das whose classical lines and instinct for undiluted traditional Odissi appealed to her. She decided to extend our stay in Puri and had Ayah and Oscar travel to Puri by train from Delhi and join us. We moved out of the comfortable hotel into more humble lodgings at a government Circuit House. But shortly after Mummy began her studies, Oscar came down with some mysterious illness and lost his voice. I was convinced he was going to die and was anxious to return to Delhi. Guru Deva Prasad Das, a timid, soft-spoken devotee of Jagannath, had at first been reluctant to teach my mother, but when he saw her determination and the risks she was willing to take, he began to take more interest and agreed to travel to Delhi to continue the lessons. Dance critics and scholars such as Dr. Fabri, Mulk Raj Anand and Mayadhar Mansinh, when he was in town, would often sit in on these classes.

Oscar survived and Debu became a part of our household in Delhi. As he came to know us better, he revealed a surprising comic side to his seemingly morose demeanour. As a young boy, he informed us, he had toured Orissa as a member of his grandfather's Jatra troupe and theatre was his first love. One night, inspired by Daddy's after-dinner Martha Graham, he took centre stage with his imitation of indigent actors auditioning for a travelling theatrical troupe. Each actor was required to recite a rousing speech by a king, urging his subjects to take up arms, march into the glory of battle and draw the enemy's blood.

"Ithay oppoman, de la Kaanchi Rajah . . . Jaago jaago . . ." He paused to translate the Oriya into Bengali which my father then translated into English. The first actor to audition was an out-of-work wrestler who punctuated his lines with push-ups and muscle flexions. Then came a toothless, doddering old man with a cane, followed by the hand-clapping, hip-wiggling hijra, or transsexual. By the time he got to the audition of a man suffering from ringworm, scratching himself uncontrollably, he had us almost crying with laughter, begging him to stop.

The Delhi dance world, members of the press and Members of Parliament from Orissa who gathered at our Sujan Singh Park flat one chilly December morning missed out on the king's valiant calls to arms. Instead Debu, dressed in a simple white dhoti with a red sash about his waist, presented an informative lecture-demonstration of his unadulterated form of Odissi dance, retaining some tribal and Tantric elements. Sceptics in the capital were converted, their minds finally open to the possibility of accepting Odissi as a viable classical dance form firmly rooted in the *Natya Shastra*.

On 19 February 1958, when the curtain went up before a packed audience at the All India Fine Arts and Crafts Theatre, the air crackled with electricity. The figure silhouetted in a filigreed pool of light moved forward languorously as Debu's shaky but fervent voice rose in prayer to Ganesh, describing the beauty and attributes of the beloved elephant-headed god.

My mother was costumed in a red silk Orissa patola dhoti and a canary yellow blouse. Chunky silver jewellery, purchased from the lanes behind the Jagannath temple, covered her wrists, arms and neck, and Haile Selassie's massive silver belt shimmered and jingled around her waist. The relatively simplified costuming, bereft of the paraphernalia worn by the dancers we saw in Puri, bequeathed Odissi with an entirely new look. My mother resembled a Konarak statue miraculously come to life.

"Last night," wrote Dr. Charles Fabri of that performance, "was an important milestone in the history of Indian dancing, for this was the first time that a professional ballerina has presented true Odissi classical dances on the stage . . . Indrani's dance reminded one of the charming dancers on the walls of the Rajarani temple of Bhuvaneshwar and the heavenly apsaras on the Sun Temple at Konarak . . . all the seductive charm of rounded liquid movements marked by exquisite grace and sinuous flowing lines."

In the 1 June 1958 issue of *The Illustrated Weekly of India* Ragini Devi wrote an article on Debu's art, illustrated by photos taken by my father, bringing an all-India attention to the art of Odissi and the guru.

16

The Trunk with the Pink Roses

My grandmother was now based in Bombay where she was struggling to complete *Dance Dialects of India*. Her letters to us were increasingly filled with accounts of the daily hardships and frustrations she confronted living on her own. The money orders my parents dispatched monthly were her sole source of income. Her Rockefeller grant money to research the book was long used up; constant snags and interruptions kept pulling her away from her ancient and temperamental typewriter. She was nearly seventy, and suffered from bouts of arthritis and heart palpitations. There were quarrels with landlords that necessitated constant changes of address. One quarrel ended with her hitting her landlord with a metal pipe. Both she and the landlord found themselves in jail, and on the front page of *Blitz*.

Ragini forgot her own troubles for a while, and put aside old animosities, when she heard from friends that Ramlal Bajpai was returning to India. On the morning of 15 November 1962 she taxied over to the Bombay Harbour to join a group of former freedom fighters who were gathered on the crowded dock to welcome him back to his homeland. At the age of eighty-two my grandfather had agreed, after some initial reluctance, to retire from his post at the Indian consulate in New York and take my mother up on her invitation to come and live with us in Delhi.

My mother had been urging Nana for years to retire and return to India. She asssured him that he would be welcome. My father had started to hunt around for a suitable ground-floor flat, so Nana could avoid climbing the flight of stairs to the Sujan Singh Park flat. We had all looked forward to having his calming presence in the household. Ragini was, of course, hurt that such an offer was never made to her. She had, in the past, balked at my mother's suggestion that she could, if she wanted, return to Minneapolis and live comfortably in her family home with her brother DeWitt and his wife. Daddy had often invited Nani to stay with us when Mummy was away on long tours, so I suspect he would not have objected greatly to her living with us. But whenever she and my mother were together in a room, fireworks would explode within minutes and the tension would permeate the entire household.

My grandfather's position in the consulate library had opened up right after Independence. Prime Minister Nehru had personally assured that as long as this freedom fighter lived, the position would be his to keep.

As Ramlal Bajpai made his way down the gangplank, looking tanned and fit from the invigorating sea voyage, Ragini ran up to garland her estranged husband, and shower him with rose petals.

He had been sceptical about returning to India but decided to give it a try, leaving open his options to return to America. The plan was for him to rest a few days in Bombay, catch up with friends, and then continue to Delhi by train. That same night Ramlal Bajpai went to bed at the home of old friends and died peacefully in his sleep.

For the first time all dance activities ceased in our family. Ragini was genuinely saddened but was able to see the beauty in his returning to his homeland to die. But my mother was inconsolable and riddled with guilt. She felt she should have gone to Bombay to receive her father. She should have insisted he return to India sooner. She wished she could have visited him in New York more often. She was looking forward to spending time with him. Their meetings over the years had been sporadic: time squeezed in during the Miss India trip to America, time squeezed in during subsequent dance tours. That her father had never set eyes on his grandson was a tragedy, magnified only by Nana dying on the day of his namesake's sixth birthday.

News of my grandfather's death reached me at my boarding school up in the mountains. I, too, had looked forward to getting reacquainted with him. Apart from his brief visit to Delhi some years earlier, I knew him mostly through his letters. The grandfather I remembered meeting was a tall, soft-spoken man with silvery white hair. Nana wore elegant American suits, a felt hat, and a miniature Indian flag in his lapel; he wrote me letters in strong bold handwriting, sent through the diplomatic pouch. These letters were usually written in Hindi, a language he had championed during the revolutionary years. He remained an ardent nationalist, yet he was a great admirer of the American way of life.

Christopher Columbus, he reminded me, came to America by accident, certain he had arrived in India. Ever since, the destiny of America and India had been inextricably interwoven. Great Yankee clippers brought back cotton, silk and spices from the East. Tea from India was dumped into Boston Harbor. Books, translations of ancient Hindu scriptures and thought, were also brought back by New England sea captains. Thoreau, the "Cosmic Yankee," had a copy of the Hindu bible, the *Bhagavad Gita*, with him on the shores of Walden Pond. His essay on the "Duty of Civil Disobedience," was taken literally by Mahatma Gandhi to rid India of the British through his campaign of Passive Resistance.

My grandfather clipped out a full page copy of the Declaration of Independence from *The New York Times* and sent it to me: " . . . that all men are created equal, that they are endowed by their creator with certain inalienable rights, that among these are Life, Liberty and the pursuit of Happiness." The Indian Declaration of

Independence drew inspiration from this document stating: "We believe it is the inalienable Right of the Indian people as of any other people to have freedom and to enjoy the fruits of their toil . . ." Nana wished I might someday come to America for my studies. But most of all he wished I would stay away from the arts and not become an artist . . . "like that Ragini Devi."

He need not have agonised. I was starting to drown in two thousand five hundred years of cultural chaos, and craved a calm orderly life. I could no longer endure the increasingly volatile spats between my parents. Their frequent separations, undoubtedly, fuelled the discord. My mother openly lamented over having married so young, and becoming a mother by the age of sixteen. She blamed her mother as well as my father. Years later, towards the end of his life, my father let it slip out that when I was a baby, my mother had negotiated with a member of Calcutta's distinguished Tagore family to give me up for adoption. I was too stunned and upset to ask for further details. Instead, to spite my mother, I cut off my long braid, that she'd always admired and had asked me to never cut, and put the matter to rest. Perhaps she was compensating for her lost childhood years, but I could sense from an early age that she had an eye for other men. It took little detective work since she was never particularly discreet about her various liaisons.

My mother had laughed off her own mother's succession of lovers and couldn't comprehend my prudishness. She always considered me old-fashioned, and jokingly called me "a one-man woman." As I grew older I began to resent these other men in her life, more and more. My father, who retaliated with women friends of his own—mostly other dancers—wondered why she didn't just pack up and leave him. When she did threaten to leave, taking both Oscar and myself with her, I turned into the queen of melodrama and managed to keep the family glued together—at least for a while. As an ultimate act of protest I ran away to boarding school.

My first taste of school in Delhi had been the Convent of Jesus and Mary. In my two years there I learned to recite the Lord's Prayer each morning, and to dance "I'm a little teapot short and stout," with one arm forming a handle and the other poised to pour. I began to develop genuine headaches after I was made to spend an entire morning in the classroom, standing in a dust bin with my face to the wall, as punishment for using a Hindi word, "almari," instead of the anglicised "almirah." I hesitated complaining to my parents since they had pulled all kinds of strings to get me into what, they were led to believe, was one of the city's finest schools. Mercifully, the pediatrician I was taken to see for my headaches, advised my parents to immediately remove me from the convent.

They eventually found the perfect fit for me at Auntie Gauba's school. Elizabeth Gauba, a German woman from Munich who dressed in saris and severe high-collar blouses, had come to India in the 1930s with her Indian husband. They had gained Nehru's friendship and gratitude during the early Congress years in Lahore when "Uncle" deserted his factories and a lucrative business in favour of the freedom movement.

It was India's scholarly, acerbic defence minister, V.K. Krishna Menon, who convinced Auntie to put her unconventional theories on education into practice by opening a school in her spacious Hailey Road flat. When I first joined the school it was simply called Auntie Gauba's school and, often, when students arrived in the morning Auntie would still be in bed correcting papers and drinking her morning tea. When she officially named the school "Shiv Niketan" we were required to assemble in the courtyard each morning before class and recite a Sanskrit sloka that began with: "Shiva Na Ma Ha." Since the water pressure to the first-floor flat was temperamental, Auntie would often be stranded, half-bathed, in the bathroom, situated just off the courtyard, and would have to conduct the prayers from inside the bathroom, yelling out "Shiva Na Ma Ha."

Although I was a little in awe of Auntie, I couldn't wait to get to school each day. The mornings were devoted to subjects like, Hindi, English, math, geography, history and science, which were mostly taught through various card games she had devised. The afternoons were devoted to writing and rehearsing plays, creating costumes and masks, puppets for puppet shows, painting and charcoal drawing, which I loved. A few of us, including my best friend who was Japanese, would get so absorbed in these activities that we sometimes stayed overnight, sleeping on charpais on Auntie's roof.

Auntie Gauba's students had included the daughters of architect Cyrus Jhabvala and novelist Ruth Jhabvala, the son of Charles and Ratna Fabri, actor Kabir Bedi and Rajiv Gandhi. Sanjay Gandhi, whose behaviour Auntie found hard to control, was invited to leave the school. Eyewitnesses report that in later years, during the Emergency when Mrs. Indira Gandhi was prime minister, Auntie was so agitated over all the power that had been bequeathed to Sanjay, that she marched into Mrs. Gandhi's office and slapped her on the face. Another time Panditji, unexpectedly, turned up during a school function and complained that he had not been invited to a play in which the normally shy Rajiv had a leading role. Auntie told him off: "Arré bhai, if I invite the grandparents as well as the parents, where am I going to seat them all?" She terrorised the other parents as well and held strong views on how they should raise their children and conduct their own lives, and was openly more partial to the fathers.

While my mother was away dancing in Europe, it was Auntie who conspired with my father and arranged to send me off to boarding school. I would have been perfectly content to continue in her school forever—sadly, her school did not cater to students beyond age twelve. Auntie did, however, take an active role in placing them in schools she considered suitable to their needs, where they could continue their formal education.

My mother was furious. But by the time she returned it was too late to change plans. The Lawrence School, Sanawar, provided the orderly life I had been craving. It was a perfect balance between the Convent of Jesus and Mary and Auntie's school. We said Grace before meals, called our teachers "Sir" and "Ma'am," and sang traditional Sanskrit slokas, interspersed with Christian hymns, during morning assembly. Indian first names were anglicised to Bambi, Bunny, Billy, Bogie, Buck.

I now recollect with shame the fun students made of a rather fine Bharata Natyam teacher who spoke English with a strong South Indian accent. I said nothing to silence them. Anyone from the South was labelled a "Madrasi" and automatically considered lacking in sophistication and social graces.

The new friends I made, became my friends for life. Their mothers were a different breed from mine. They had their hair done at the beauty parlour, wore flowered chiffon saris imported from France, and threw bridge parties where they served chicken patties and pineapple pastries from Wengers. They played golf at the Delhi Golf Club and tennis at the Gymkhana. Some smoked cigarettes and either drove their own cars or were driven by chauffeurs.

We, too, aped Western culture. We discovered boys. During our summer and winter vacations back in Delhi we organised and attended parties where we drank Cokes, and cha-cha'd and foxtrotted and rock 'n rolled to Xavier Cougat, Nat King Cole, Bill Hailey and the Comets and Elvis Presley. We poured ourselves into skintight salwaar kameezes, and backcombed our hair into towering beehives. We smeared our lips with Revlon's Persian Melon, and drowned ourselves in Shocking Schiaparelli and other perfumes borrowed from our mothers.

Ayah was suspicious of these new friends. They would make me eat pork in their homes, she claimed. She subjected me to breath tests, and had me blow into her face whenever I returned home from having coffee with friends at the Volga or La Boheme. She had, of course, no idea what ham or bacon smelled like and couldn't tell the difference even when I had been guilty of that crime. My parents' friends were viewed with equal contempt. Two poverty-stricken painters and a journalist made a habit of dropping by almost every evening just before dinner time. "Don't these people have homes of their own?" she would comment loudly when she let them in, knowing fully well they'd be back the next day, whether or not my parents had other plans.

One hot summer day a freckled red-haired man named Arthur Godfrey threw our Sujan Singh Park flat into complete turmoil. An American TV personality, Godfrey had already televised my mother dancing in front of the richly carved Hindu stone pillars out at the Qutb Minar complex. To add a personal touch, he thought it would be fitting to interview her at home.

The proposed title of the Indian segment of The Arthur Godfrey Show was "Jungle Rhythms of India." But the actual jungle of India proved to be more of a hindrance and not the type of authenticity he was seeking. As Mr. Godfrey, dressed in a flowered bush-shirt, chatted with my mother in front of the TV cameras, the sensitive audio equipment kept picking up the chirping of a vociferous family of sparrows that had taken up residence in the crown of a ferocious, elaborately carved mask of Ravana, made even more ferocious by his coiffeur of dried grass and twigs draped over his bulging eyes. Mr. Godfrey stopped the taping and demanded that Ravana and his tenants be evicted from the room.

My mother let him know politely, but firmly, that it was quite out of the question.

Those sparrows were respected members of our household; so much so that during the peak of the blistering summer heat the ceiling fans would be switched off while fledgling sparrows took flying lessons from their parents.

Mr. Godfrey's technicians spent the rest of the morning devising an ingenious soundproof contraption which boxed in the demon king of Lanka and silenced his feathered friends temporarily. Ayah was assigned the responsibility of supplying the frazzled television host and his technical crew with glass after glass of lemon squash, which had to be prepared with water that was first boiled for twenty minutes in the "foreign" kettle, then cooled with ice cubes made earlier in the day with the foreign water. The poor foreigners, not able to comprehend any of her snide remarks about gutless people who could only stomach boiled water, continued to smile sweetly at her, and thanked her profusely for her labour.

By that time the Chinese ambience of the household had been supplanted by a more American one. A set of unbreakable dishes, patterned with autumn leaves, that Mummy had picked up during one of her tours to the US, replaced the delicate porcelain bowls from China. Our wardrobe went through a similar Americanisation. Oscar's cowboy costume, and my Jackie Kennedy–like dress came from Macy's department store in New York—a store where one could buy absolutely everything in the world.

In the fall of 1961 my mother was invited by The Asia Society in New York to tour the US with her troupe. She took with her three musicians from Bangalore—a vocalist, Lokiah, a flautist, Srinivasa Murthy, and a drummer, Seshadri. Her dancers included Baliram, a darkly handsome, statuesque Bharata Natyam dancer, who was originally from Nepal, her Kuchipudi guru, Korada Narasimha Rao, and Deva Prasad Das, who also doubled as Odissi accompanist. The high point of the tour was an invitation from Jawarharlal Nehru, who was visiting the US, to perform at the Indian embassy in Washington, at a special Diwali celebration he was hosting for President and Mrs. Kennedy. In Nehru's honour, Jacqueline Kennedy wore a dress with a bodice encrusted with red gems to match Nehru's signature red rose in his lapel. The glittering event was attended by Indira Gandhi, President Kennedy, his mother Rose Kennedy, his sister Mrs. Sargeant Shriver, his brother Ted Kennedy, Jacqueline Kennedy's sister Princess Lee Radziwell, her mother and stepfather, Mr. and Mrs. Hugh Auchincloss, and ambassador B.K. Nehru and his wife. A small makeshift stage, with a tiny screen to serve as the greenroom, had been set up for the dancers. What the audience witnessed was a dazzling performance of three styles of dance—Bharata Natyam, Kuchipudi and Odissi. What the audience didn't see was all the mayhem behind the screen as the four dancers tried to make elaborate costume changes. Gossip circulated that John F. Kennedy had tried, through embassy officials, to set up a date with my mother—she never confirmed or denied these rumours. The next day the newspapers in the US and in India were filled with pictures of my mother smiling up at the handsome, young American president.

So it was particularly shocking, when a few weeks later headlines blazed across papers, including *The New York Times*, *The Shreveport Times* and *The Charlotte Observer*, stating: "Indian Dancer Hits Race Curb In South," "Hindu Troupe Refused Service, Cancels Show," "Snubbed Indian Dancer Says, 'We Wouldn't Insult People.'"

While touring the South, restaurants in Charlotte, North Carolina, and Bossier City, Louisiana, refused to serve four of her artists food. The owner of the Eatwell Grill said that the other customers had complained that they would leave if "Negroes" were served, but offered to serve them food in the kitchen. The same thing happened at the Kickapoo restaurant in Bossier City. My mother cancelled all performances in those towns and threatened to cancel the entire tour. State Department officials rushed to apologise for this treatment to artists who had just performed for President Kennedy. The Reverend Billy Graham, who was visiting India with a group of American churchmen, took personal responsibility for the behaviour of his fellow Americans and wrote my father a letter of apology for the incident. Privately, when the artists, confused further by segregated rest rooms, asked my mother, "Amma which bathroom should we use?" she suggested they do whatever they needed to do right on the signs that read: "White" or "Colored."

There was further excitement on that tour when John Martin, of *The New York Times*, singled out Narasimha Rao as an "outstanding character dancer." As a result of this accolade—coming on the heels of being adjudged "the best male dancer from any country" at the Theatre des Nations dance festival in Paris—Korada was bashed up by the other male dancers and left with a bloody nose.

The Andhra Lion, as Korada was known, was a character on and off stage. When he returned to Elluru, his village in Andhra, after one tour, we received a letter from him written on his new stationery. The letterhead said something like, "Korada Narasimha Rao, dancer, teacher, M.A., NY." When Daddy later asked him how he'd found time to do his Master's in New York, Korada grinned and said "NY" simply stood for "Not Yet." When he came to the house to give my mother lessons he generally dressed in simple white dhotis and kurta. But he was once spotted walking along Janpath in full make-up— lipstick, tweezed eyebrows, nail polish, jewellery and magenta shawl. When we teased him, he swore he was respectably married and had a son back home to prove it.

My mother returned home from her tours invariably broke. She'd shout up to Ayah and ask her to dip into the bazaar money and throw her down the taxi fare.

"Hah! Miss India has returned from foreign," Ayah would screech, loud enough for all our Sujan Singh Park neighbours to hear. "My famous memsahib has plenty of money to throw away on all these gurus and baja-wallahs, but never enough to pay for taxis."

Ayah, in her brusque manner, had all along managed to hold us together. But, things slowly began to disintegrate. I was done with school, agonising over what to become when I grew up. I'd been fairly casual about my studies, so I surprised myself when I ended up receiving a first division for my final Senior Cambridge exam— though my parents, who had never pressured me over my studies, didn't seem particularly surprised by the result. I was at a loose end, that horrible summer of 1964. It was the summer "Mummy" was abridged to "Ma." It was the summer our Siamese cat vanished, my brother came down with chickenpox, and the summer Pandit Nehru died, despondent over China's invasion of India's border regions. And it was the summer we lost Ayah.

For close to eighteen years it was Ayah's daily routine to wake up before five every morning to light the coal-stove. She would prepare little ping pong–sized balls, made out of charcoal residue and water, which she'd set out to dry on the veranda. She had devised a system of baking potatoes and custards and roasting mutton by placing hot coals on lids of pots sealed with a paste made from flour and water.

My mother decided it was time to modernise the kitchen and had the coal-pits cemented and replaced with an efficient new gas range.

The gas made Ayah nauseous. She refused to go anywhere near it. What had been wrong with her cooking all these years? She had heard no one complain.

The tension and emotions kept mounting. One morning the electric hot plate she had taken to using blew a fuse before breakfast could be cooked.

"Why don't you try cooking sometime!" she screamed at my mother. And after smashing some pots and pans in the kitchen, and bursting into tears, Ayah packed her small trunk with the pink roses, which had always been stored under our bed, and marched out of the door. I ran down Cornwallis Road, crying after her, begging her to change her mind, but she wouldn't turn around. She just kept marching till she was out of sight.

17

Le Club Solitaire

Following Ayah's departure our household started to rapidly disintegrate. My mother's scheme to ship me off to Paris for studies was devious, circuitous and came as a complete surprise. Winning the art prize at Sanawar had convinced my family and teachers, especially Auntie Gauba, that I was destined to become a famous painter, India's next Amrita Shergil. The Bharata Natyam classes I was attending three times a week, with a guru descended from Chokalingam Pillai's Pandanallur lineage, were more to oblige my grandmother and mother than to fulfil any burning desire of my own to become a dancer. Dressing up in costumes and taking centre stage was one thing, but the tortuous demands on the body and the herculean discipline was quite another. Nani saw through my lack of enthusiasm and stopped pushing me towards perfection—so long as I didn't give up dance entirely. Besides, she herself possessed a talent for drawing and painting which had, for the most part, remained unexplored.

In retrospect, I suspect more than my aptitude for painting was involved in my mother's decision to send me to Paris. At the time I was shamelessly in pursuit of a rather dashing Punjabi boy whose ardour did not match mine. How my parents unearthed my closely guarded secret remains a mystery, since we never discussed the matter. But I found out through my network of girlfriends that they actually disapproved of one of Delhi's most eligible young men, and considered him an unprincipled playboy who would leave me with a broken heart.

More than that, my absence from home was to clear the way for my mother to finally pack her bags and move with Oscar to a flat of her own.

My obligatory adolescent rebellion was confined mostly to fantasies of leading a luxurious life of leisure. I envisioned spending the rest of my life being driven around in chauffeured cars, shopping for beautiful saris, throwing scintillating dinner parties, reading novels, painting my toenails.

For the time being, it turned out, all I was destined to paint were canvases. The College of Art in Delhi failed to inspire me any more than the dance classes. Months of toiling through tedious mechanical drawing and lettering came to a happy close around the breakfast table one winter morning, when my mother threw out the idea of my studying painting at the École Nationalé des Beaux Arts in Paris. I couldn't believe what I heard. I was either dreaming it, or there had to be a catch. There was a catch. I would have to depart almost immediately, keep the Paris part of my trip a secret, and briefly resurrect my career as a tanpura player.

My knowledge of the Paris art world came primarily from books like *Moulin Rouge* and *Lust For Life*. The idea of studying painting in Paris, living a Bohemian life in some garret, dressing in black, sitting in cafés smoking cigarettes, sipping absinthe, and discussing the meaning of life till the early hours of the morning, appealed to my tortured state of mind. The walls of my bedroom were already plastered with reproductions of paintings by Degas, Cezanne, Matisse and Van Gogh.

Those were days when "P Form" regulations and foreign exchange restrictions made foreign travel almost impossible for the average Indian. Only those on a scholarship or students with families solvent enough to buy foreign exchange on the black market could afford to travel abroad for studies . . . as could students with parents as imaginatively resourceful as mine.

Arrangements for my mother to travel to Hong Kong and Kuala Lumpur with her group of musicians had just crystallised. The Indian Government would issue me a passport and a ten-day "P Form" to travel to Hong Kong and Kuala Lumpur as a tanpura-playing member of her troupe.

There was barely time to think or pack or shop or say any goodbyes. Once our BOAC 707 jet was safely in the air my mother ordered splits of French champagne to celebrate my "escape." It was six in the morning and seemed deliciously reckless and sinful. It was only appropriate to be reading *Angelique*, a trashy gutter-to-palace-to-gutter novel about some French nobleman's mistress, and ripping out pages I'd read and passing them on to my mother who couldn't wait for me to finish the book.

I strummed my way through Hong Kong and Kuala Lumpur in a complete fog. After a short holiday visiting some Indian friends in Bangkok, my mother put me on a KLM flight to Paris via Karachi and Amsterdam, this being one of the flights out of Bangkok that did not make a stop in India where, since my exit permit had expired, I would have been deplaned and probably prohibited from ever leaving India again.

I landed at Orly on 5 February 1965, a grey overcast day. Akbar Padamsee, an Indian painter and friend of my parents', met me at the terminal at Les Invalides and settled me in a hotel on Rue du Sommerard, where other Indians frequently stayed. The reality of being completely alone for the first time in my life suddenly hit. I began to agonise about everything I could agonise over. Was this perhaps the hotel my grandmother had skipped out on without paying her bill? Was that same concierge who had plied my mother with hot chocolate still lurking nearby? Were the police still waiting for her to pay up? There was little family resemblance. My face was genuinely brown; no one could connect me to those ancestral escapades.

Still, I thought it wise to maintain a low profile. I memorised the streets of the Quartier Latin from a map of Paris my father had saved from one of his official trips abroad. I knew I could walk past the Cluny Museum, down Boulevard St. Michel to Place St. Michel, then proceed along the banks of the Seine until I reached my destination— the École Nationalé des Beaux Arts on Rue Bonaparte. Yet I was anxious about venturing beyond the vicinity of the Hotel Marignan. The hotel remained a safe haven in spite of the concierge and his wife who constantly found fault with everything I did. I was not permitted to keep food in my room, I was not to spend more than ten minutes in the shower down the hall, the bidet was not meant for washing saris. The stairs leading up to my tiny third-floor room were dark even during the day. I lived in fear of bumping into an almost-seven-foot-tall African flute player, who always smiled at me, and I prayed the minute-light would remain turned on till I could reach the next switch.

I filled up on baguette halves, butter, apricot jam and the strong, foamy coffee Madame Keniger slammed on the table in the small dining room each morning. I had never in my life eaten at a restaurant alone, so at the risk of arousing Madame's ire, I'd sneak into my room crisp red apples, cubes of La Vache Qui Rit and tubes of Nestle's Sweetened Condensed Milk. Sitting alone in some café sipping absinthe and smoking would remain a fantasy. It was some time before I mustered the courage to walk into a self-service restaurant near the Jardin de Luxembourg.

Aside from ubiquitous fruits and cheeses, nothing in the display case looked safe to eat. I was afraid I'd end up eating a rabbit or a horse or some obscure organ. I'd been warned against Gallic incivility so I was taken aback when a well-dressed gentleman seated next to me leaned over, said he spoke some English, and offered to help translate the menu.

It would have been most ill-mannered, after he had rescued me from starvation by introducing me to Oeuf Plat Jambon and pomme-frittes, to decline his offer to take me on a little tour of Paris. He mentioned his name, which was preceded by some preposition, as I climbed nervously into his car. He drove me by the Place de La

Concorde, the Louvre, Notre Dame, Charlemagne's statue, the Ile St. Louis, and pointed out the posh Tour d'Argent restaurant.

He invited me for dinner the next evening and offered to show me Paris by night. After his many kindnesses I found it hard to decline his invitation to his face. Prior to my escape from Delhi, Daddy had recruited Charles Fabri, who was apparently well attuned to the tribal customs of the European male, to give me a little pep talk and some advice on how to protect myself. Charles was most earnest and cautioned me "to beware of lurid foreigners bent on seducing innocent eighteen-year-olds." The following evening I went into hiding in my room. At the appointed hour, while the concierge continued to buzz me on the intercom, I kept quiet and, in lieu of some elaborate preparation of duck, settled down to my habitual repast of apples, La Vache Qui Rit and Nestlé's Condensed Milk.

Paris by night could not have been more beautiful than Paris in the early-morning hours. The only people about were street cleaners and waiters in long aprons, sweeping sidewalk cafés and setting out chairs and tables stacked the night before. The rapidly rising sun bathed the fairy-tale turrets of the Conciergerie, and the dome of the Institut de France and the Louvre across the river, in a pale pink glow. I walked the mentally rehearsed route along the Seine towards the Beaux Arts, rolled up samples of my canvases tucked under my arms.

After filling out a million forms, and having my canvases evaluated, I was assigned an atelier. The all-important *Carte d'Etudiant*, now in my possession, satisfied a gruff concierge who permitted me to enter a studio. The door shut behind me with finality. I felt like a prisoner in the Bastille when I heard the concierge turn the key and march away. Professor Tondu's class was already in progress. I quietly took a seat in the back. But soon my head began to spin. I felt a surge of nausea. The gamy stench of infrequently washed underarms mingled with fumes of Gauloise and marijuana permeated the overly heated room. I found I was allergic to marijuana. And when I picked up my piece of charcoal to draw what the other students were drawing, I was mortified to discover our subject was a flabby middle-aged man wearing only a walrus moustache.

I stared at a blank sheet of paper, too embarrassed to even lift my head, until a female model replaced him several days later.

When the time came for me to move out of the Hotel Marignan, into a more affordable Catholic hostel for young women, I asked the concierge to fetch a taxi. He exploded, threw his hands up in the air and spewed forth a high-speed tirade. I had lived all these months under his roof, he and his wife had treated me like a daughter, and now I insult them by asking for a taxi!

I was flabbergasted.

Monsieur Keniger grabbed my luggage, threw it into his blue Renault, drove me over to the Foyer de Jeune Fille on Rue des Bernadins, and carried the suitcases up to my room on the fourth floor. If I encountered any problems, he said roughly, I was to contact him or his wife immediately.

It would take time to unravel the French character. Vive La France!

The cultural sections of both the French embassy in Delhi and the Indian embassy in Paris had pulled all the necessary strings to arrange for me to be awarded a French government scholarship. I soon fell into a happy routine of walking every morning to the Beaux Arts and painting still lifes and drawing naked, though inanimate, Greek and Roman statues at the Louvre. Yet the spectre of dance had not been shaken off. It had followed me to Paris and crept insidiously back into my life.

I augmented the modest French government bourse by taking on odd jobs requiring an Indian woman in a sari. I promoted Indian tea, worked as a hostess in the Indian pavilion at the annual Foire de Paris, and did some modelling. When the Indian Tourist Office invited me to dance for a group of tourists on their way to India, I jumped at the offer. I would be paid fifty francs, almost a month's rent, for ten minutes of work. When the director of the tourist office first mentioned "Le Club Solitaire," where the performance was to take place, I presumed it had something to do with diamonds or the Orient.

I pulled myself out of mothballs, brushed up the proper version of Natanam Adinar, the dance of Shiva, to recorded music, and threw together a costume. A young French woman who performed Kathak was to share the evening with me.

Milena and I arrived at Le Club Solitaire together. We were led to a back room where we put the finishing touches to our costume and make-up. The audience was already in place so there was no chance to check out the performance area. A quick survey of the space, from behind a curtain, told me all I needed to know.

"Solitaire," I realised with a sinking heart, meant "single." This was a "singles" club, a dark cheap little cabaret. Men and women were noisily milling about as if at a cocktail party, clinking glasses of whisky and champagne. The dance floor was in front of a bandstand.

All at once a vision of Shiva loomed before me, his third eye threatening to reduce me to ashes. He was flanked by my grandmother and mother, their eyes flashing disapproval as well. I quickly started changing out of my costume. They would forgive me many sins, I knew, but they'd never forgive my performing sacred temple dances in a sleazy nightclub!

Milena was surprised.

"I didn't think you were so religious!"

I was not religious. For me all religions were jumbled into one confusing mess. But getting into costume, standing on stage, dancing, I suddenly realised, was sacred.

Milena was a far better sport and rescued the evening from turning into a fiasco with her courtly, elegant Kathak dances. My refusal to perform worked the patron of the club into a wild rage. He eyed me up and down as if I were some belly dancer with leprosy, and called me an "arrogant Hindou." I returned home with my self-respect intact, but minus fifty precious francs.

Other opportunities to perform in more respectable venues and earn some badly needed cash, began to crop up with regularity. After a performance at the annual "Les Peuples Qui Chantent" festival at the Sorbonne, an American painter friend I had looked up to declared rather callously that he thought I danced better than I painted. I didn't mind. The sound of applause had already begun to grow addictive.

The second year of my scholarship was coming to an end. The idea of dance, a form different from Indian dance, was beginning to take shape in my head. Before returning to India, what I really wanted, deep in my heart, was to travel to New York and study American modern dance with Martha Graham. The image of my father flailing himself on the floor had remained strongly embedded in my memory. But Martha Graham herself had made a deeper impression on me when I saw her perform with her company in Delhi in 1955. At a reception after the performance, I had the great privilege of presenting her with a bouquet of roses. Although just eight years old at the time, I knew I was in the presence of a genius.

My parents thought I had gone mad. They had only just come back together again and celebrated their reunion by moving into a new, more spacious government flat on Shah Jahan Road that my father had designed. Their brief separation had devastated me, but I realised from questions he would write and ask me about her and questions she would ask about him that the situation wouldn't last long. Once their second honeymoon was over I knew they would revert back to their old ways, but the bond between them, volatile as it was, was unshakeable.

Letters began to fly between Paris and Delhi. My mother and father were convinced a painter's life was better suited to my anxiety-prone temperament than a dancer's. I didn't dance badly, but it was not my major gift. My strengths and shortcomings were suddenly being scrutinised under a microscope.

Although they were apprehensive, Ma and Daddy eventually resigned themselves to the idea of my going to New York.

New York City, they wrote, could be fearful on first contact, especially in summer when it was hot and deserted. However, it could grow on one rapidly and deeply. My grandfather had wished I would go to New York for studies. He believed in the American way of life, learning and work. My grandmother, who had rubbed dark make-up all over her skin and insisted she was a Kashmiri Hindu, was violently anti-American and opposed to my going and studying American dance. Funny, they said, how each had chosen the other's country and way of life.

My parents turned nostalgic imagining me in New York and laughed over the fact that they were both, in all important aspects of their lives, products of the US.

18

A Family Affair

I landed at the John F. Kennedy International Airport on 4 July 1967 with forty dollars in my purse, a three-month tourist visa, and a burning desire to study dance with Martha Graham. I had little idea how I'd achieve this, but felt it was an auspicious omen to arrive in America on that date, since my grandfather, unsure of his exact date of birth, chose to celebrate his birthday on 4 July, the Independence Day of his adopted country.

Relieved to have survived the arduous queues and anxiety of passing through immigration, I scanned the international arrival lounge for my American painter friend from Paris who had promised to meet me and temporarily house me with his family, but all I could see crawling through the crowds were oversized policemen who looked like human arsenals: their hips bulging with pistols, clubs, handcuffs, and walkie-talkies spewing static. Everyone seemed to be in a desperate hurry. Impatient. Pushing. Shoving. If Ted hadn't turned up when he did, I'm certain I'd have been gunned down or trampled to death.

A good portion of my forty dollars was swallowed up by a hair-raising taxi ride from the airport to the Bronx. Our fearless driver, who clearly resented any vehicle edging ahead of him, screeched our cab to a halt in front of a modest two-storey brick house off Gun Hill Road. Ted's father was glued to a game of baseball on a giant colour TV set, his mother was in the garden picking faded blooms off her rose bushes. After the usual polite introductions and some awkward expressions of my gratitude for their generous hospitality to a strange foreigner, his mother led me upstairs and installed me in her bright, airy sewing room.

I removed my crumpled silk sari and treated myself to the luxury of American plumbing. It was a hot, muggy day, so after a long refreshing shower, I changed into a cotton sari. I was eagerly looking forward to the special "cook-out" planned in celebration of the American Independence day.

When I joined the other guests on the patio, I realised right away that I was inappropriately dressed. Everyone, even the women, were dressed most casually in shorts, T-shirts and sneakers. My enthusiasm began to fizzle. The bottle of French champagne I had brought my hosts remained unopened; we settled instead for six-packs of "Bud."

My celluloid image of New York had been of sleek skyscrapers, with views of the East River and Fifty-Ninth Street Bridge; sunken living rooms with wall-to-wall carpeting, penthouses with fully stocked bars that swung magically out of walls, and sophisticated ladies, in black strapless gowns, sipping iced martinis; William Holden courting Audrey Hepburn.

This delicious bourgeois decadence kept eluding me. Later that evening Ted, a writer friend of his—another American refugee from Paris—and I boarded a dirty noisy subway that thundered down to West Fourth Street, to Greenwich Village, to the haunts of O. Henry, Jackson Pollock, Allen Ginsburg, the Beatniks—none of whom seemed to be around any more. We ended up at El Faros, a Spanish restaurant on Horatio Street.

To enter into the spirit of the city, I ordered a Manhattan. It was sweet, sickening and awful. It began to rain, everything turned dank and depressing, sidewalk vents spewed noxious fumes, and my heart plummeted through the metal grating into the bowels of the city.

Forsaking Paris for this? I had made a dreadful mistake.

My grandfather was not with me that Fourth of July but I felt his presence. His spirit would protect me, I knew, even though I wanted to become a dancer . . . "like that Ragini Devi."

A few days later I made my way to the Graham School on East 63rd Street and introduced myself to Martha Graham's sister, Geordie. She was seated in a small upstairs office with Charlie, her shaggy brown poodle. Yes, yes, she had been expecting me. My mother had already alerted the school and Miss Graham, in fact all of New York, about my arrival and my desire to study modern dance.

Martha Graham had seen my mother dance at Jacob's Pillow in the early sixties and went out of her way to make me feel welcome. The school arranged for my student visa and, following an open audition, offered me a scholarship that covered the tuition. Promises that friends of my parents had made about helping me find employment, failed to materialise. But I soon picked up odd jobs—working in an antique shop in the Greenwich Village, a ladies' dress shop in the East Fifties, and Sona, an Indian handicrafts store.

I walked into the beginner class, dressed in the brand new black tights and leotard I had purchased from Capezio's, and looked in the mirror. Every lump and curve on my body was exposed; I felt naked.

The students rose when a teacher (not Miss Graham) entered the studio. She directed us to sit on the floor.

"Knees out, soles of the feet together, forehead touching the feet and bounce . . . and one, and two, and three and four . . . "

In the daily beginner class I began to move my body in an entirely new way. I ran to see every possible performance the Martha Graham Company presented in New York. I studied films of Graham's mentor, Ruth St. Denis; her Dance of Radha, Incense, White Jade. Graham's dances weren't as exotic and decorative as Ruth St. Denis's. But what they shared in common were central female figures of great mystery and power: Ruth St. Denis expressed the joy, beauty, and the evocation of life; Graham focused on psychological struggles and human movement.

The actual movements felt alien to me, but the spirit was not alien; there was an underlying sanctity that was connected to the Hindu gods. Dance was an expression of the divine. This divinity, our centre, is revealed when the dancer is in complete harmony with the universe; the dancer becomes an intermediary between the gods and mortals.

Graham was then in her seventies, battling arthritis and alcohol, and though she still performed with her company, she mostly left the teaching to her dancers. But every so often she would sweep into the studio and correct our postures by shoving us in the ribs, or straightening the spine, and then depart after declaring something profound. "Wherever a dancer stands ready," she would remind us, "that spot is holy ground."

Martha Graham made me aware of my centre. This central force, I began to see, was universal. It kept appearing in unpredictable places and unexpected performances. Dance had come full circle for me.

Physically, my dance technique benefited from the intensive Graham training, which I kept up for three years, but spiritually it made me gravitate back to my Indian dance roots. I began to realise that I had taken Indian dance for granted. I had taken my dance studies with my grandmother, my mother, and other Indian gurus for granted. I had lost valuable time. When my mother came to the US to tour with her company in 1968, it was as if I were seeing her dance for the first time, especially her Odissi. As a child I had been blind to the spirituality, austerity and playfulness of Indian dance. I was now ready to return to it.

For the duration of her two US tours in 1968, I was recruited back into the troupe as tanpura player, and dance student. A sterile motel room in the Hollywood Hawaiian in Los Angeles was not the ideal setting. Yet it was there, on the carpeted floor of our room, that my mother began to teach me the opening movements of Sringara Lahiri. The dance of Goddess Parvati, expressing her love for Shiva in a gentle lyrical mode, had been taught to her by Ragini, many years earlier.

Now she devoted every spare moment—whether in an airport lounge, on the plane, backstage at the Greek Theatre, in a TV studio between tapings of the Smothers Brothers' Comedy Hour, on the train to Poughkeepsie, even by the entrance of the BMT subway in

New York—to teaching me dances from her own repertoire. She critiqued me, notated the dances, illustrated them with little matchstick figures, and had her musicians record the music. Even after she returned to India the instructions continued by mail. She hounded me with her zeal. It was overwhelming. In 1969 during the Graham school summer break, I returned to Delhi to study extensively with Deva Prasad Das, and to continue training with my mother.

On a cold January day in 1970 I felt emboldened enough to give my first full solo performance at The Education Theatre at New York University. Thanks mostly to the efforts of my mother's American tour-cum-stage manager and lighting designer, Frank Wicks, every seat was taken by friends, Indian dance lovers, and hordes of "flower children" and devotees of the current cult hero of the psychedelic masses, Ravi Shankar, whose tours, including the now-legendary Woodstock Festival, were also managed by Frank. This performance was, a few days later, followed by a tour of Europe capped off by a command performance at the palace in Brussels for King Baudouin and Queen Fabiola of Belgium.

But, sadly, as our family gained one new dancer, it lost another. Unknown to me at the time, on the day of my debut performance in New York, my father, back in Delhi, was photographing my mother and some of her dancers, using the ruins of Hauz Khas as a backdrop. In what was a bizarre accident for someone as cautious as my father, he apparently stepped backwards as the Kathak dance brothers, Durga Lal and Devi Lal, were performing a pirouette for him to photograph. He lost his footing and fell several feet to the ground below and sustained a spinal injury which left him a paraplegic for life—no longer able to entertain us with his famous takeoff on Martha Graham.

I believe the fall was something more than just an accident. A week earlier a visiting French architect had fallen from the same spot and been killed. Daddy's older sister who had rushed to Delhi from Calcutta insisted it was the work of a "jallali bazurg," a restless spirit. Her theory was not dismissed as yet another superstition handed down from Dadi: when he looked back at the whole episode, Daddy recalled a moonlight picnic, hosted at Hauz Khas by Steb and Chester Bowles,

US ambassador to India and his wife, for an American dance troupe. He couldn't resist Steb's after-dinner invitation to perform his Martha Graham for the guests and decided it would be more dramatic to make his entrance from the interior of a nearby, darkened tomb. Just as he leapt out of the entrance of the tomb a stooped-over old man with a flaming red beard followed him out of the tomb screaming abuses at him in Urdu for defiling a grave. The Hauz Khas complex had been built as a madrasa, a school, and Daddy was now certain this red-bearded apparition was the ghost of the architect.

I had been kept in the dark as to the gravity of his injuries and discouraged from rushing to Delhi in the middle of my European tour. But an emotional letter from my old mentor, Auntie Gauba, gave me a clearer picture and filled me with remorse that I had not gone to him. "Your father's terrible accident," she wrote, "was the strangest thing we ever saw happening. The way the whole Rahman family reacted to accepting the situation and combat the illness was just extraordinary. Each of them, man, woman and child stood revealed to each other and to all as personalities of infinite force and tenderness . . . The end result I saw last Sunday when I saw your father, smilingly, struggle to learn to walk again . . . this is nothing short of a miracle. He has made up his mind to sign up as chief architect and walk to his office and I'm dead sure he'll make it. Your mother's nursing of your father is an unforgettable spectacle. Day and night for four months, nearly always at the edge of a nervous breakdown, she managed to be twenty Hindu wives all rolled into one. Oscar was a great comfort and a pillar of strength to both of them. Daddy once told me with tears in his eyes 'people are all so good to me. I always thought everybody hated me, but now it seems this wasn't true.' And your Mummy wept almost into the telephone and said how much she loved him: 'it was because of this illness that he has revealed himself to me as the wonderful person he really is.' "

My mother had put aside her dancing and turned down an enticing tour to Osaka. But in mid-May, placing Daddy's older sister, Apa, and her husband, Dulha Bhai, in charge, she decided to go ahead with a tour to France, taking Oscar with her.

On 12 June 1970 under the supervision and care of his doctor and nursing sister at the Safdarjung Hospital, Daddy limped into his new office with the help of two walking sticks to take up his position as chief architect. An architect friend drove him in his car, along with Apa, who insisted on accompanying her brother to the office. He was overwhelmed, and nervous, to find a crowd of about seventy-five or so from the architectural department—some to welcome him and some out of curiosity—waiting in front of the entrance lobby with garlands. He presided over a two-and-a-half-hour meeting, then returned to the hospital exhausted.

In spite of all her fortitude, I don't believe my mother ever recovered fully from the shock of this experience and found it increasingly difficult to take care of him. She began to drink heavily, and took solace in her dancing and looked forward to her tours to America with her company of dancers and musicians.

In time I graduated from playing the tanpura for my mother to actually dancing with her. My affiliation with her troupe was further cemented when, following a long wonderful friendship and brief courtship, I married her lanky American tour manager.

Frank soon added the title of producer-impresario to his list of credentials. Our tiny Mott Street apartment doubled as a booking office where Frank and I licked envelopes, mailed flyers across the country, confirmed bookings, begged friends to house and feed the artists whenever necessary. One tour led to another. When my mother returned to Delhi between tours the lessons continued. She began to send me dances by mail, dance notations, matchstick figures, dance music on cassette tapes. I taught myself the dances from her little match-stick drawings and practised, practised, practised in various rented studios around the city. She taught me her Odissi items, Mohini Attam, more Bharata Natyam, and Kuchipudi items including her famous Mandodari Shabdam, the dance of the frog princess.

The pattern was set for the next few years: my mother and I dancing, and Frank producing, stage managing, designing lights, and running the sound. Our touring entourage mushroomed with the birth of our two sons, Habib and Wardreath. No more daughters to carry on the gharana. I was secretly relieved. There was nothing more exhilarating than throwing one's body and soul into a dance and nothing more agonising than trying to uphold the expectations and high standards set by my mother and grandmother.

Touring as a mother-daughter team had its ups and downs. When my mother watched me dance my solos, I was always tense and felt she was waiting for me to make a mistake. There would be notes slipped under my motel room door giving me corrections, telling me what items I could dance for a particular performance, and notes telling me what costume I could or could not wear. If I received a good mention in a review, I ran the risk of being called an "upstart." At the same time there was nothing my mother wouldn't teach me. She gave and gave and gave most generously and was constantly pushing me to perfection. And when we'd go flying across the stage together, in our final tillana, it was sheer exhilaration.

After bouncing some years between our New York apartment and a cottage on a tranquil Maine island, we chose to continue our dance activities and our nesting in Maine. It had never been my intention to leave India permanently. But insidiously little roots had taken hold. I felt like a spreading banyan tree with a portion of my roots in India and a portion in America.

19

Curtain Call

The family was now scattered all over. I was living in Maine with Frank and our two boys. My brother was in New Haven working towards a Master's degree in design at Yale. My mother was based in New York, performing and teaching at Juilliard, NYU and Harvard during the summers. She returned to Delhi for a month or so each winter to visit with my father, who was now retired but still continuing with freelance architectural work.

My grandmother, who was in her eighties, was living alone in Bombay; her health was failing and her housing continued to be a problem. It was a dilemma for my mother who was struggling herself to make ends meet in New York. We thought of bringing Ragini back to America, but we all knew that would take a miracle. How would she survive? Where would she live? Medical services were prohibitive. Our microscopic income from performance fees, teaching fees, and occasional grants could not support another soul. We avoided high medical insurance payments and exorbitant doctor bills by simply staying fit and praying for good health.

Litia Namoura, a former dancer, who had performed with Ragini in her early days in New York, suggested we approach the Actors' Fund Home in New Jersey, a residence for retired performing artists. Getting past long waiting lists and being accepted into the home, we knew, would be a hurdle but convincing Nani to go into a home filled with aged Americans would be even harder. She had not ventured out of India for thirty years. She was a stranger to America and did not regard herself as an American.

My mother approached Martha Graham who without a moments' hesitation shot off a persuasive letter to the Actors' Fund of America on my grandmother's behalf. Ragini, she wrote, had been known to her as a dancer of eminence for many years. She was numbered among those visionary beings who helped to pioneer the revival of the dance of India in the thirties. It had been brought to her attention that Ragini Devi was in dire circumstances and very much wished to return to her home in America and reside at the Actors' Home in Englewood, New Jersey. Her residence there would not only bring to her great peace of mind but would give her the environment in which to complete her book on Indian music. She recommended that Ragini be given whatever assistance she needed to become a resident— not only for what she now wished to contribute but for what, Graham felt, she had contributed in the past.

In a similar appeal, John Martin, former dance critic of *The New York Times*, reminded the Actors' Home that it was just fifty years ago that he had reviewed Ragini's first book on Indian dance, and praised her contribution to dance, both in India and in America. She was no longer young and in need of assistance.

I wrote my grandmother a persuasive letter assuring her that Frank's elderly parents, who lived in New Jersey quite close to the Actors' Home, would keep an eye on her and invite her often to their place for home-cooked meals. They had accepted me with open arms and were, by now, quite accustomed to their son's odd relatives and friends. They would be happy to take her shopping, drive her into the city to see performances, meet friends, and go to parties. She would not be locked up and put out to pasture. This finally gave my grandmother the courage to leave Bombay. Frank himself had won her over when, on one of his trips to India with an American modern dance company, he had visited Ragini in Bombay and presented her with a bottle of Johnnie Walker.

There were, as yet, other hurdles to overcome. She had to be repatriated as an American before she could enter the country. When she appeared at the American Consulate in Bombay she pulled out several expired passports and dumped them on top of the counter. The woman in charge was scandalised. She scolded her and advised her to quickly put away all the different passports. As an American she was not permitted all these other nationalities. Had she not registered her name with the police when she first arrived in India?

"What do you mean register my name with the police?" she cried in disbelief. "I'm Ragini Devi. Everyone in Bombay knows me. People bow to me on the streets!"

A group of Parsi ladies who ran the Time and Talents Club, a cultural organisation for self-employed women, organised a farewell party for Ragini. The two Vakil sisters, on hearing Ragini was still without a plane ticket, immediately took up a collection and wrote a blank cheque to Air India. They had never forgotten Ragini's performances with Gopinath in the thirties. The very first performance they attended had turned them into avid patrons of the arts.

The last person to bid Ragini Devi farewell that evening was Harindranath Chattopadhyaya, still handsome with a shock of white hair and scholarly spectacles. She accepted a beautiful silk sari from him and departed with a coy smile and a sparkle dancing in her eyes.

Litia Namoura and my mother were at JFK to receive Ragini one bitterly cold day in February 1978. She staggered off the plane, clutching onto her battered old typewriter. Neither Ragini nor the typewriter looked as if they'd survive that first night in New York.

A sunny private room with an attached bath at the Actors' Fund Home, three full meals a day, free medical care, monthly social security cheques, and a devoted staff, restored her back to good health. Initially she voiced complaints about the home. The other dancers living there were mostly vaudeville artists and not intellectually stimulating. Never-ending tales of their touring days put her right to sleep. The consumption of tobacco and liquor on the premises was forbidden.

But she was soon drawn into the world outside. My mother organised parties in New York and reunions with old dance cronies. Ram, the name my brother now insisted everyone use, came often from New Haven. And Frank senior mixed a perfect dry martini. Nani even agreed to visit us on our island in Maine. It was to have been a relaxing time: eating home-cooked Indian food, sitting by the fire, getting better acquainted with her great-grandsons. But moments after she walked in the door, she pulled out some ancient, crumbling dance notes, and began teaching me the ashtapadi she had learnt from Jetti Tayamma in Mysore a millennium ago. I dropped everything and concentrated on learning the dance. Dance and dance-related activities, I knew by now, were the only things that kept my grandmother's motor running. The birthday and Valentine cards she'd send her great-grandsons usually had, along with a five-dollar bill, some old dance photo from her glamourous days glued into it. I tried to get her talking about her past, about what had really drawn her to India and to Indian dance—but I was served the same line as everyone else about her being a Hindu in a previous incarnation.

My mother and I were preparing for our annual New York performance. Frank was busy shooting off press releases, mailing flyers, trying to sell tickets. A few weeks before the performance Walter Terry, the dance critic, telephoned and demanded to know why Ragini Devi was not performing with us as well. If Martha Graham and Ruth St. Denis could have danced as long as they did, why shouldn't Ragini? Nani was eighty-six; it had been decades since she had last performed. After some initial hesitation and an attack of nerves, Ragini took to the idea and agreed to perform a brief passage of mime.

When the curtain came down on my grandmother that evening of 29 September 1979, she turned to me, overwhelmed no doubt by the thunderous applause, and asked anxiously:

"Should I dance that again?"

"That won't be necessary, Nani," snapped my mother, eager to get on with the performance.

Ragini had danced to her favourite poem from Jayadeva's *Gita Govinda*. My mother sang and I strummed the strings of the tanpura while Ragini Devi portrayed, through gesture and mime, the young, petulant Radha rejecting her wayward lover, Krishna:

"Having struggled through the night, she appeared withered by the arrow of love. She rebuked her lover as he touched her feet, pleading forgiveness . . .
Go Madhava! Go Krishna! Don't plead your deceitful words with me.
Go after her, she will dispel your anguish."

Frank lifted my grandmother and helped her into the wings. My mother and I continued with the performance.

At the end of that performance Ragini Devi was offered one more opportunity to savour the addictive applause when she joined us onstage for our final bow. The Education Theatre at New York University was sold out, and as friends and colleagues, including many of the great names in American dance, rose to pay tribute to her, an oddly familiar voice cut through the applause screaming "Nani! Nani! Nani!"

Running down the aisle was our old Ayah. It had been fifteen years since she had packed her trunk and marched out on us. She had not seen my grandmother in twenty-five years.

I was dumbfounded—torn between wanting to hug her with happiness and wanting to hit her for abandoning us. She had, we soon learned, been brought to New York a few months earlier by the Bangladeshi ambassador to the United Nations and his wife to care for their little girl. Knowing my mother, brother and I were in the country, this diminutive illiterate woman, who spoke no English, had wandered around Central Park asking other Bengali and Hindi-speaking domestics where she could find us. A servant of the Indian consul general finally helped her track us down.

She scrambled right onto the stage just as my brother was placing a garland around my grandmother's neck. He managed to drag Ayah off the stage as discreetly as he could. Unperturbed by all the commotion, Nani drew her cream-coloured silk sari around her shoulders and acknowledged the standing ovation graciously.

"This concert," she said, "is the climax of my life, which is drawing to a close. I am happy to see the pure tradition safeguarded by my daughter Indrani and my granddaughter Sukanya."

I tried to hold back the tears streaming down my face, thankful my prayers for a normal life had remained unanswered.

I had fulfilled my karma. I could now face those celestial nymphs in Indra's heaven with a clear conscience.

Postscript

A modest grant in 1981 from the National Endowment for the Arts, in Washington, D.C., provided me the opportunity to travel to Bangalore for intensive dance studies with the eminent Bharata Natyam guru, Tanjore Kittappa Pillai. I stretched the fund to its limits and flew to India with Frank and our two young sons, moving into a simple but comfortable guesthouse across from the Bangalore Club on Residency Road.

Bangalore was quite changed from the early fifties when I had spent a crazy month there with my grandmother and Ayah. Brigade Road was barely recognisable, and Nani's old bungalow torn down and replaced with one of the high-rises that now dominated the city's skyline. The one comforting link to the past was the tribe of intrepid monkeys who caused perpetual havoc, swinging from one papaya tree to another, and dropping the unripened fruit into the water tanks on our roof, much to the glee of the boys.

My mother had arranged for me to study with Kittappa, whom she had studied with years earlier, and understood my yearning to immerse myself in dance training in the orthodox style: eight hours a day of private lessons, seven days a week, no days off for weekends, Christmas, New Year, nothing. Yet I sensed I had let her down by going to another teacher at this stage of our professional relationship. Happily an opportunity to melt the friction somewhat presented itself over breakfast one morning in December when I picked up the local daily paper. On the front page, just above a news item on the death by drowning of actress Natalie Wood, was an announcement that Indrani Rahman had been selected to receive that year's Sangeet Natak Akademi award for her contribution to dance. That recognition, overdue as it was, considering her reputation and seniority on India's dance spectrum, would I knew, please her enormously. I picked up the phone and booked a call to New York. She was, of course, thrilled by the news and right after talking to me phoned Ragini at the Actor's Home. It was perhaps the result of getting excited by the good news, combined by the subsequent argument my mother and grandmother had over some trivial matter, but during the conversation Ragini's speech became garbled and the phone went dead. The staff at the Home called back to report that Ragini had suffered a stroke and was being rushed by ambulance to the Englewood Hospital.

Ragini's final performance, using Kathakali hand gestures, was to convey to her daughter that she was going to die. She was going to die where, she had remarked on an earlier stay at the hospital, her grandson-in-law, Frank, had been born. She was eighty-eight when she passed away on 22 January 1981, with my mother holding her hand. She was cremated in New Jersey according to Hindu rites performed by Ram Patwardhan, protégé and friend of her husband, Ramlal Bajpai.

A few days following her death, I went over to the Theosophical Centre on 6 St. John's Road, walked in the shade of the tamarind and jacaranda trees and pondered on the incredible life and journey of the young American woman and her newborn baby who had been given refuge here some fifty years earlier.

In March 1982, when my mother officially received the Sangeet
Natak Akademi award, she simultaneously accepted a posthumous
award for Ragini, presented to her by Kamala Devi Chattopadhyaya.

Considering Indrani and Ragini's largely bumpy relationship, my
father, who was in New York at the time of Nani's death, was
bewildered at the extent of my mother's grief. And considering his
even bumpier relationship with my mother, he might have been
equally bewildered at her reaction to his own death in December
1995 at the age of eighty. After years of coping heroically as a
paraplegic and amputee, he died peacefully at home in Delhi, in his
son's arms. Some days earlier he received news that he was to be
awarded the first Lifetime Achievement award in architecture and
was busy putting together his bio and photographs for the press.

I didn't see it at the time, but his death was the beginning of my
mother's end, both physically and emotionally. Later that year, when
she and Frank and I returned to Delhi to join my brother for the
posthumous award ceremony, we were convinced she'd had too much
to drink and was being melodramatic when she claimed that this
would be her last time in India.

Without ceremony, she had stopped performing around 1989, but
continued, as she had since 1976, to teach her students at Juilliard.
She devoted the last decade or so of her life to presenting performances
by promising young dancers in New York, often in her tiny living
room, but more frequently booking them at prestigious venues including
the Lincoln Center Out of Doors Festival, the Ravinia Festival in
Chicago, and for three consecutive years, opening the Sylvia and
Danny Kaye Play House season with her presentation: Indrani, Dancers
and Musicians from India. Her goal was to continue to educate and
convert audiences to different forms of Indian classical dance. "Once
they're hooked," she'd say, "they'll appreciate a two-hour solo
performance of Bharata Natyam or Odissi or Kathak." But these
performances took their toll on her as well, physically and financially.

Her untimely death from a massive stroke in New York on
5 February 1999 was a shock to all. Since her miraculous recovery
from a stroke she had suffered in the fall, I was convinced she was
indestructible and would live forever. On her deathbed I draped her

in her first Odissi costume, a red patola sari; she looked much younger than her sixty-eight years and appeared to be resting serenely before jumping into her next ambitious project.

In a letter of condolence President of India K.R. Narayanan wrote: "It is impossible to think of Indrani as being no more, so synonymous with life and energy and creativity that she was. Her understanding of Indian dance and music was as deep as her rendering of nritya was authentic. Admired internationally for her artistry as well as her intellect, Indrani Rahman will be keenly missed. Her influence on contemporary dance and on generations of artists in India and abroad will, however, remain indelible . . . "

Deborah Jowitt of the *Village Voice* wrote, " . . . based in New York for much of every year, she danced, lectured, taught and sponsored other performers. Indian dancers tend to be territorial. Not Indrani. I'd pick up the phone and hear her lilting voice explain that a splendid exponent of such-and-such style was in town for a while, and she'd just arranged a little showing in someone's studio. Many Asian dancers in New York owe their reputations to her. When we met, she was often on the run, slightly out of breath, always merry, always gracious . . . Luckily, spirits like hers don't disappear; they linger in our memories and fortify us."

At her funeral, art collector and former director of the National School of Drama, Ebrahim Alkazi, quoted Dylan Thomas, and spoke eloquently of her "going gently into that good night." Other close friends like architect Cyrus Jhabvala, spoke with humour of her excessive bossiness and of being told exactly what to order and what to eat at the Penang Restaurant where he and his wife, the novelist, Ruth Jhabvala, had lunched with her two days before the fatal stroke. James Ivory, the filmmaker, also recalled Indrani as being bossy, insisting on directing him as he filmed her dancing at the Qutb in the early sixties, an experience that set the precedent for Ivory to always take his directorial cues from his actors.

In my last conversation with my mother, the day before she lapsed into a coma, she was helping me draw up a guest-list for a ceremony at the Asia Society where she was to be presented with a Lifetime Achievement award. The event, held as scheduled, was turned into a memorial during which I read chapters from this book and accepted the award on her behalf.

As I look at it, "spirits like hers don't disappear; they linger in our memories and fortify us.". . . Through her dance, Indrani will live with us forever.